INCORRIGIBLE

Velma Demerson

Wilfrid Laurier University Press

We acknowledge the support of the Canada Council for the Arts for our publishing program. We acknowledge the financial support of the Government of Canada through the Book Publishing Industry Development Program for our publishing activities. We acknowledge the Government of Ontario through the Ontario Media Development Corporation's Ontario Book Initiative.

Library and Archives Canada Cataloguing in Publication Data

Demerson, Velma, 1920–
Incorrigible / Velma Demerson

(Life writing series)
ISBN 0-88920-444-6

1. Demerson, Velma, 1920–   2. Women prisoners—Ontario—Biography.
3. Interracial dating—Ontario.   I. Title.   II. Series.

HV9505.D44A3 2004   365'.43'092   C2004-906735-4

© 2004 Velma Demerson
Second printing 2005

Cover design by P.J. Woodland. Photograph of Harry Yip by C.D. Hoy, used with kind permission of Barkerville Historic Town, BC (photo P1574).

Text design by C. Bonas-Taylor.

Throughout this text fictional names have been used for inmates of the Toronto Industrial Refuge and the Andrew Mercer Reformatory for Females. Any resemblance to actual persons, living or dead, is entirely coincidental. The names of government and institutional officials are as stated.

Every reasonable effort has been made to acquire permission for copyright material used in this text, and to acknowledge all such indebtedness accurately. Any errors and omissions called to the publisher's attention will be corrected in future printings.

∞
Printed in Canada

Order from:
Wilfrid Laurier University Press
Wilfrid Laurier University
Waterloo, Ontario, Canada N2L 3C5
www.wlupress.wlu.ca

I dedicate this book to
my beloved son Harry Yip

— I would like to join forces with all those who believe that the past and the present are indivisible.

$\mathcal{C}$HAPTER 1

$\mathcal{A}$s the car turns into the driveway, I see the Andrew Mercer Reformatory for Females as a dark formidable fortress pencilled black against the white sky. The enormous structure with its jutting turrets appears to stretch an entire city block. It casts a shadow over the grassy exterior extending to a wide spiked iron fence and onto the street beyond. The tall steeple gives a church-like appearance but the numerous iron-barred windows embedded in the dark stone exterior frighten me.

The building is distant from the street but as we draw near I can see the women who were at the Belmont Home with me leave the other car and move toward, then up the stairs. They are partly hidden by the hulking figures of two men.

During the drive from the Home, we three girls squeezed into the back seat sat unmoving, still absorbing the shock of sudden removal from our restrictive but reasonably safe haven. Only Adelaide's sniffling could be heard. Her tears weren't allayed when Miss Pollack assured us of well-being in our new quarters. The foreboding appearance of the reformatory seems to justify Adelaide's apprehension. She has stopped crying and is staring at the looming reformatory that awaits us.

$\mathcal{T}$he car stops and the two plainclothes guards sitting in the front seat get out. One of the men opens the door. As we emerge from the back seat, we're aware that the two men are within arm's length, watching us warily. The small pale-faced girl who had been sitting next to me is practically lifted off her feet by one overzealous guard. The other seizes my arm in a tight vise. Satisfied with having contained his prey, he reaches out with his other hand and fastens his grip onto Adelaide. Her eyes are still glued to the stark prison confronting

1

us. I want to shake her out of her trance but can't get my arms to move. My limbs feel leaden and my body as inert as the stone edifice we're about to enter.

Adding to my feeling of helplessness is some obscure premonition, an instinct that something dreadful could occur in such a sinister place. My throat feels taut. I feel isolated, apart. Fear envelops me. I feel totally alone.

The two men remain crushingly close as they direct us up the stone steps, through the gothic arch of the entrance to the door, and ring the bell. Without delay, as if watching from the window, a woman with grey-ing hair and wearing a brown dress with a broach opens the door. Her appearance suggests she's the superintendent and is expecting us. Her attention is directed towards the men who have escorted us and with whom she will conduct the business of our transfer. This time I'm not entering the office or being greeted by the superintendent as I was at the Home. This time I'm entering an institution where all personal recognition has been dispensed with. This sudden realization triggers an immediate identification with all the women who preceded me and stood on this very spot. It's becoming horribly clear that my life is for-feit to a still unknown but punitive monster—the state. All movement, all time, even my very thoughts are being consumed. I feel naked, shamed, and defenceless.

The entrance hall is immense with shining hardwood floors. From it extends a spiral stairway with strong banisters. I envision the steps extending all the way up to a high-raftered ceiling—a tower.

There's a wide doorway to the right. To the left is a hallway. There are no furnishings, not a clock or a chair. The absence of a clock disturbs me as I contemplate timeless, meaningless days. The enormous space diminishes me. I imagine the warmth and comfort I've known being replaced with rigid austerity. A sinking feeling overwhelms me as I envis-age every bit of control over my life being taken away.

Aside from low voices engaged in the solemn rite of conveying human cargo, there are no sounds. We stand in the hall outside the open door of the office under the men's watchful eye, brutally aware that talking may not be tolerated. Having completed their task, our escorts are impa-tient to leave and eager to turn us over to a tall older woman in a white uniform, who says tersely, "Come with me."

She leads us to a room, holds the door open, and bids us enter. We are surprised to hear the door click locked behind us.

My mind spins back to try and pinpoint the exact moment that this nightmare began.

It's 1939 and I am eighteen years old.

CHAPTER 2

*A*fter our brusque reception we find ourselves installed in a large cloakroom where we are immediately introduced to the place's discipline. "There's to be no talking," a matron says. We're relieved to find the room filled with familiar faces from the Home. I try counting those present but give up when I reach forty. It appears that a good number of the older Belmont girls aren't here. One of the first batch of transferred girls whispers to me, "Miss Pollock was crying when she said goodbye." We stand about waiting. We're instructed to discard our Belmont attire and change into Mercer clothing. "Put the clothes you have on in a neat pile in the corner." The matron designates a place on the spotless floor. We undress quietly.

I can see that the girls ahead of me in line are getting large cotton dresses, aprons, underwear, white cotton stockings, and black shoes. When my turn comes, I put on a large faded old-fashioned dress. It's extremely wide and reaches my ankles. However, when I put on the full apron with its long ties I can see that it will hold the dress in, making it look like it almost fits. The thick cotton stockings are about two inches too long at the toes but are easily stuffed into the shoes, which are also several sizes too large.

Each girl has quickly been handed a bundle without reference to size. We learn that we can expect to be issued standard Mercer attire in our own size later. What we've been given is the garb provided to all new inmates, to be worn for the first few weeks. In the months to come we are always able to recognize a new inmate by her initiation clothing. To girls already in a state of anxiety, the code of silence and humiliating dress further the subjugation. We are young women, aware of fashion. We know that large cotton dresses and wide aprons belong to a past era of drudgery on the farm.

A matron passes out food on old tin pie plates. I'm beginning to suspect that inmates will never have pie. Pie is probably served to staff. Large tin cups resembling measuring cups are provided for black tea that has large leaves floating in it. An older inmate pours the tea from a chipped enamel jug. We eat standing up.

A matron unlocks the door and says, "Get into an orderly file." She directs us toward the open door, then walks behind, ferrying us along the wide corridor to the hallway where we came in. She seems annoyed at our confused behaviour and is relieved to pass us over to another matron who is standing at the foot of the stairway, monitoring the women who emerge one by one from the dining room. They have had supper and are heading upstairs to their cells. In their uniforms they are almost indistinguishable. I'm astounded at the numbers, maybe two hundred. The matrons look harassed and ill-tempered. We forty-seven incorrigible girls from the Belmont Home probably interfere with the routine and cause additional work. The women slow down as they reach the stairs. The matron is pushing me into line as I try frantically to remain with my friends. As the women move forward, I'm swept up the stairs. Two matrons are trying to keep order. A matron cries out shrilly, "Keep in single file!" I feel myself drawn into the company of silent women and emulate their actions. All that can be heard are the raising of our feet in unison as we ascend the high steps. An eerie feeling overcomes me—the realization that I'm about to become one of this voiceless tribe. On the second floor landing another matron is waiting. She directs me to turn left to the east wing. I join the others going in the same direction. The matron follows as we pass through the oval entrance to the ward, which is a corridor perhaps six feet wide with about twenty cells. They're all on one side facing the windows. The windows are too high to see out but are nevertheless barred. There's a large unreachable box that looks like a loudspeaker fastened to the wall above a cell. No sound ever comes out of it. The floors are hardwood, darkened from long usage.

The matron points to the cell I will occupy. All the cells look the same but I'm supposed to remember the location of the one I'm allotted. I enter and am dismayed to find a windowless enclosure, arched like a honeycomb and built in with bricks. It's about seven feet long and four feet wide with an iron-barred door. The thought of being locked into such claustrophobic quarters is overwhelming. I stretch my arms and place the palms of my hands against the rough interior. The small cell reinforces my feelings that I'm shrinking. My restricted space is in sharp contrast to the prison's enormity.

A bare light bulb protrudes from the side of the wall above a narrow cot with coiled springs. On the cot waiting to be made up are a thin cotton mattress, sheets, two coarse grey blankets, a pillow, and a pillow slip. A white towel and roll of toilet paper are placed on a chair.

At the foot of the bed is a small basin with a cold water tap. There's a bar of Ivory soap, a toothbrush, and a tin of toothpowder. A covered white enamel pail to be used as a toilet sits on the floor.

My legs ache from standing around and ascending the stairs. I cannot absorb more of my wicked situation, don't even have the energy to arrange the sheets. I lie a blanket on the springs, close my eyes, and collapse. The awful thought seizes me that I am now a Mercer girl and so have no personal expectations.

I hear a voice and open my eyes. "You're not allowed to lie on your bed in the daytime."[1] I see a girl with straight brown hair standing outside my cell, looking at me. She knows I'm a new girl by the clothes I'm wearing.

I go into the corridor. Girls are standing around talking in the corridor. Why don't they take the chairs out of their cells to sit on? Perhaps they're not allowed to.

"Where's the matron?" I ask the girl.

"She'll be back in about half an hour. We're having free time before we're locked in our cells for twelve hours."

"Twelve hours," I say ruefully.

"Most of the girls in this ward are first offenders except maybe one or two," she tells me. "Someone said that a bunch of girls came in from a Home." She wants to be friendly, she's curious. Her way of taking a new girl under her wing is the same as when I arrived at the Belmont, but still, I'm wary of my surroundings and suspicious of why the girls are here.

My cell isn't far from the entrance but I thought I saw another Belmont girl as we came in. I walk down the corridor, peering into each cell. At the very end, not far from the toilets, I find Victoria sitting on the chair in her cell. I wouldn't think they could send a fourteen-year-old to a reformatory.

Victoria looks like an alabaster doll with her pale skin, fair hair, and light blue eyes. We concur that we're the only Belmont girls on the ward. Victoria looks tired and speaks so softly I can hardly hear her. She has endured so much pain she has little to say. I don't know how a girl with epilepsy can survive here.

I look closely at the Mercer girls. None appears to be pregnant. I must be the only pregnant girl on the ward. Who can I talk to, even during our short interludes?

I return to my cell and hurriedly make my bed before the matron returns. I hear the sound of keys jingling as she approaches. She bids us to enter our cells and says firmly, "There's to be no talking." We are quick to obey.

The matron begins the laborious task of retrieving the cell keys and locking each of us in. The padlocks on our doors have to be opened individually—which is why prison inspectors call the place a fire trap.

The lights are left on in our cells although there's nothing to read and nothing to do. Eventually, the lights go off. It's not completely dark, there's some light from the hall. During the night I hear the soft steps of a matron passing through with her flashlight, casting the beams quickly over the sleepless women.

—

The following morning I hear a loud cowbell. I see the matron through the bars of my cell door, swinging a brown cow bell back and forth. She admonishes us to hurry up and get dressed. Then, one by one, commencing with the furthest from the entrance, she unlocks each cell door.

We hear the sound of a whistle and, with military precision, step out of our cells holding our pails. The matron remains behind the girls, directing each one individually to hurry towards the toilets at the end of the corridor to dump her waste. As each girl is quickly returning, another is directed forward.

Back in our cells we wash, brush our teeth, and make our beds. The ritual having been completed, at another signal we step out of our cells and line up for the trek downstairs for breakfast. The women from the other wards are also entering the dining room so we await our turn.

As we enter the huge dining room I perceive, facing us at the far wall, a middle-aged woman sitting on a raised chair that resembles a throne. She is sitting upright, her forearms resting on the curved arms of the chair, her head diminished by the high ornate backrest. A girl whispers to me that this is Miss Milne, the superintendent. I decide she's the same person who admitted me to the reformatory.

A matron standing at the entrance watches the women leave the line and go to their regular tables. She breaks away from her station at the door and shows me where to sit. We are six at our table and I sit down with girls I don't know. They look at me, noting my pregnant condition. I can't see the other Belmont girls.

It's an immense room with a large number of round bare oak tables, each seating six or more. The tables are divided into the right and left sides of the room with a wide space in between. The women march down the centre to locate their table. The Belmont girls are told at which tables to sit; henceforth we will remember which one it is. On the left-hand side, in an extended part of the room adjacent to the kitchen, is the food-serving area behind which a few women are standing. The superintendent rises from her seat to say grace and we rise accordingly, then follow her actions as she sits down. Immediately, girls scurry about bringing plates of food that they place before us. My table is on the right-hand side and not easily seen by Miss Milne from her perch. There are no matrons about so we're able to whisper.

Providing so many girls with their proper place in the dining room seems to be a problem. We need to be separated and distributed among the general population so that close associations are broken down. There is also the matter of age. First offenders are preferably seated together.

We're having breakfast. Large half-slices of bread are piled high on a dish in the middle of the table. The bread is coarse and sugarless. It's a staple, there at every meal, and we can eat as much of it as we want. Big loaves are baked in the Mercer kitchen—by older women I surmise. It's likely that women in for breach of the liquor laws would be older experienced cooks; their sentences are not long, and they wouldn't need as much close supervision as the young girls. At each place is a white bowl containing a quarter cup of blue-tinged skim milk for porridge. An older inmate passes our table with a wooden bucket of oatmeal porridge. One girl accepts it. I'm told that it doesn't taste good without sugar so let it pass.

Because I'm pregnant, the girls pour their milk into my bowl. An inmate passes with a large enamel jug. I hold out my cup to accept the black tea.

The superintendent watches us as we eat. Then she tinkles a small bell to indicate that it's time to get up from our seats.

—

*A*ll the Belmont girls are seeing the doctor. After leaving the dining room, we're directed up the steep stairs to the doctor's clinic on the third floor. Off a long wide corridor with polished hardwood floors is the doctor's examining room. The matron passes out white cotton tops to be tied in the back and white cotton crotchless pants that cover only our legs. We put on the hospital garb and place our clothes in a pile on the floor. The matron orders us to form a line leading to the door of the medical room. The door is opened by the doctor who takes charge.

Dr. Edna Guest is a woman with short hair; I think she's in her fifties. Around her head and extending behind her ears is a black band at least an inch wide. She's wearing a long white hospital coat.

The door is left open and she tells us to follow the line right around the door into the examining room. The room is barely large enough to accommodate more than a few of us and we stand with our backs to the cabinet and shelves. We face the hospital table.

At the end of the table are metal foot stirrups about two feet apart. The doctor sits in front of the stirrups with her back to the window at the rear of the building. She's wearing rubber gloves.

I place myself near the front of the line next to my best friend Sue who's in a very late stage of pregnancy. The doctor gets up from her seat and says, "Now I want to show you how to get on the table to save time." She gives a demonstration and sits down. Each girl gets on the table, puts each foot in the stirrups, and the doctor inserts a speculum into the girl's vagina, presumably taking smears. Venereal disease is reported to be epidemic and there's extensive advertising and even films dispensing information on it.

The fact that we've already been examined doesn't spare us. Belmont Home health records are seemingly insufficient. Some of the girls must have been in the home for nearly two years. This is my third internal examination since my arrest.

A second girl gets on the table and is quickly dispensed with. Sue climbs onto the table next. The doctor decides to check her state of pregnancy. She moves the speculum about at various angles to get a better look, turning it to the far right in Sue's body. Sue winces and starts crying, unrestrained. The doctor, undeterred from her examination by Sue's discomfort, glances over at us. She gauges our reaction and discipline as we stand watching helplessly. Finally Sue, harried and tearful, gets off the table and I quickly climb on.

The doctor says angrily, "I told you how to get on the table correctly! Get down and stand over there in the corner." I stand with eyes toward the wall in a corner on the other side of the table. She's just turned me into a naughty child.

After examining two more girls, the doctor tells me to get back on the table. Examinations proceed at a fast pace. I don't recall anyone taking our names. We have to be processed, dressed, and downstairs in the dining room for our noon meal. We've quickly learned to be silent and obedient in the presence of this doctor. She's been in the military, no doubt about it.

The following week, along with the other girls, I undergo the same internal examination. This time we remain waiting in the hallway and the doctor's assistant opens the clinic door and calls out each girl's name.

We see Miss McGrath, a short grey-haired nurse, in the hallway and tell her we watched one another being examined the previous week. She says, "I wouldn't have permitted it if I had been here." I gather from her remark a certain disrespect for Dr. Guest's practice but how she might have prevented it is a mystery. Miss McGrath is a registered nurse. We know this by the black band on her nurse's cap. She doesn't assist Dr. Guest during internal treatments. This task is performed by Miss Allison, a tall woman with dark hair—perhaps in her twenties or thirties. The girls tell me that Miss Allison is the only Mercer attendant acting as medical assistant. For some reason she wasn't present during the initial examination of the Belmont girls.

*J*n the afternoon, after our initial visit to the doctor and after lunch, we Belmont girls assemble at the wide entrance to the dining room and form a line to be directed to our work stations. We crowd into a factory located on ground level and are told to take seats at any one of the thirty-three power sewing machines. It seems that all of those chosen for factory work are Belmont girls. The factory is called "Mercer Industries Ltd."[2]

The instructor and matron is Miss Miles, a severe-looking elderly lady. She sits at a long table behind us, her back to the windows that afford all the light. She's very strict and we must maintain full attention to our task. There's definitely no talking, though we can get up from our machines and use the factory toilet nearby without permission.

We learn to operate our machine with a knee press, which draws the material forward as it sews. The machine is noisy and rickety. It must be awfully old. Our first assignment is hemming pre-cut towelling. We pick up a bundle of white towelling and when hemming is complete we place the towels on Miss Miles's table for inspection and pick up another bundle. Our hours are 8:00 AM to 5:00 PM. The pay is six cents a day.

Because there's insufficient sewing space for all the Belmont girls, I suspect that some, like Mercer girls, will work in the laundry, clean toilets, scrub floors, and do kitchen work, or even wash the girls' night pails.

—

I'm being summoned to the austere visiting room to see my mother. She says, "I see you've been moved—I went to the Belmont Home and was told the Home had been closed down. There was nothing in the papers about it." If she feels anything about my transfer from a large house to a formidable institution, she's not showing it. But she must have felt at least a pang of distress when she saw this building. Did she ever imagine she would visit her daughter in such a place? What demons is she hiding? Her presence here must cut into her inborn English pride. She would have to ask for permission to see her daughter. Does she feel guilty about her involvement in my arrest? She is no longer a mother in charge; her role has been usurped by the state. She has locked herself into a position that demeans her as well as me.

I remember how she grimaced and gritted her teeth when she used to talk about the plight of frail old ladies, half-starved and beaten by self-righteous authoritarian matrons in English poorhouses. She has always feared submission to authority. I know she doesn't want to upset me or herself by mentioning the unpleasant physical aspects of my imprisonment. Now my mother, always so bent on revenge against my father, has been caught in her own trap.

—

*W*e Belmont girls have been here for about a week and we're having our half-hour exercise time in the yard. Because we're in separate wards and at different dining-room tables, this is the only time we can speak to one another. Some of the girls are standing grouped together. Their stance and expression indicate a momentous discussion is in progress. I join them. A girl known as Marion, probably in her twenties, is bitterly denouncing her transfer to the Mercer. "My aunt came to visit me—she said she went to a lawyer to try to get me out. The judge sentenced me to the Belmont Home, not to the Mercer Reformatory! And how about the others who were left behind? Are they still at the Belmont or what?"

"I'll bet those girls were kept behind to do the laundry for the old folks' homes on Belmont Street," says Adelaide.

Marion resumes. "My aunt said the lawyer looked it up and found that the law was changed a couple of months ago. It used to be that only unmanageable girls could be sent from a home to the Mercer, but now anybody can be sent here."[3]

"There was a protest at City Hall—it was in the newspapers," says one girl. "The matrons and a labour group were opposed to the move."

"My mother went over to the Belmont Home and they told her I'd been sent here. She didn't know ahead of time or she might have tried to get me out too," a small freckle-faced girl joins in.

Marion continues. "My aunt said the newspaper reported there were too many girls in the Belmont Home who hadn't gone through court and they should be in a provincial institution."[4]

Hadn't gone through court? I'm thinking that's all the more reason they shouldn't be here.

"It's not fair," says Marion.

Some days later I find Marion sitting alone on the sparse grass in the yard. She seems less perturbed than when I'd seen her last. I ask, "Have you heard anything more from your aunt?"

Marion looks hesitant. After a few moments, she looks around to be sure no one can hear and then speaks quietly. "My aunt says her lawyer could get in trouble if it was known—she's not supposed to tell anyone. You must promise me not to tell any of the other girls. This has to be just between the two of us."

"Sure," I say. "Of course!"

"Well, my aunt's lawyer is a close friend of Mr. Humphries, the deputy attorney general. Mr. Humphries told her lawyer that young women should never have been put into the Belmont Home, let alone transferred to the Mercer Reformatory. All the women had been charged with 'incorrigible,' a children's offence. But at sixteen years old we became adults and would have to commit a criminal offence to be arrested. 'Incorrigible' isn't a criminal offence."

"The Belmont Home and the Good Shepherd's Home for Catholic girls at West Lodge Avenue in Parkdale are not homes—they're really industrial refuges for young women from fifteen to thirty-five years. My aunt looked in the city directory and it says 'Good Shepherd's *Refuge.*'"

"So," I say, "Are they trying to rectify a mistake—are the girls from the Good Shepherd's going to be transferred to the Mercer too?"

"I would think so but there's been a mistake—we weren't supposed to be sent to a 'house of correction' in the first place. The judges who sentenced us believed they were sending us to a home for wayward girls for protection, not to a prison."

"What's a house of correction?"

"The Mercer Reformatory is a prison where one who has sinned must suffer for her sins. The Belmont Home is a place for wayward girls. It's for training us to find jobs when we leave.[5] The Belmont Home is a charitable institution. It accepts donations for the girls. I don't think anyone would give donations to the Mercer."

A few days later I look for Marion. I ask a Belmont girl in the yard. "Has anyone seen Marion?" No one has seen Marion around for a couple of days. She must have gotten out.

—

*E*ach noon we receive our one big meal of the day. There's meat, potatoes, vegetables, and gravy. On Fridays we have fish and on Sundays, beans and baloney. The noon meal is our main staple and it's the one to which we're entitled to have second helpings. For second helpings, we hold our dish over our heads and an inmate takes it and returns it with the extra food. We are now using proper dishes and cups.

Supper is a cold meal, sometimes a bowl of yellow cornstarch pudding or tapioca, which we refer to as "fish eyes." The sugar in the pudding is the only sugar we receive. This is the one meal when we each receive a small pat of butter.

The initial shock of arrival has abated and I'm becoming more observant. My curiosity focuses on the reputed brothel keepers. I see them coming into the dining room after we are all seated. They are the last inmates to enter and the first to leave. Their table is apart, on the other side of the aisle at a somewhat greater distance from the door than I am, but I can see them fairly well. There are no tables within several feet of them. No one will ever have the opportunity to speak to them. We neither pass them in the corridors nor see them in the yard during our free time after dinner. It's reasoned that these bawdy house operators might entice a girl to work for them when she gets out.

One of the women fascinates me. Kitty Cat Macdonald with her upswept fair hair and voluptuous figure swings her hips defiantly as she enters and leaves the dining room. She's aware she's being watched. The mere fact of being a repeater of various offences would not warrant any particular attention, however, as the wife of a well-known gangster, Mickey Macdonald, she shares his notoriety. Mickey is presently being interrogated before a packed courthouse on a murder charge. The four women at the table are quarantined as being dangerous to public morals. They smile at each other as if a big joke is in progress.

Because most of the women in the Mercer have barely passed out of elementary school, movies depicting a gangster's moll singing in a nightclub can reflect the upward mobility some women may aspire to. Gangsters who escaped from poor beginnings to acquire powerful economic freedom is a popular theme in films.

It's a holiday but I don't know why. It may be to celebrate the visit to Canada of King George VI and Queen Elizabeth who passed through recently. The newspapers have been reporting this glorious occasion for months. We're permitted to receive a box of food from a relative. It's a sunny day and we sit on the sparse grass edge of the Mercer yard and eat our treats. I don't know that the king generously cuts a month off some inmates' sentences.

My mother, who is inclined to be creative, has brought me a nice box of sandwiches and cakes. As our names are called, we go up to receive our package. I feel sorry for some of the older women who don't get a box but I don't know them and lack the initiative to share. A few Polish or Ukrainian women who have found one another are sitting together speaking their own language.

While the Belmont girls are in for being "incorrigible," I learn that many of the Mercer inmates are in for "vagrancy."[6] A good number of women are in for breach of the liquor laws with sentences of about three months. The women don't mind letting anyone know that being in the Mercer is an inconvenience.

The yard is surrounded by a high fence and the women walk around the oblong dirt path. I look up. Framed in a window just below a turret is an emaciated creature who looks like a witch. She's wearing the old Mercer initiation clothes. I'm relieved to be wearing the regular uniform—a pinstriped dress with short sleeves. The woman is looking down at us but I don't wave or acknowledge her. I don't tell anyone she's there because it's of no importance. She's probably a drug addict—why otherwise is she there? A drug addict is a sinister being.

J never waken ahead of time, only with the jarring sound of the bell. I'm so tired. Someone said that the lights go out at ten o'clock. I want to sleep earlier but the bare light bulb is glaring down and we're not allowed to cover it. I pull the bedclothes over my head. The windows are never opened; ventilation comes from the entrance to the ward.

Suddenly I hear loud clanging and girls screaming. I get up and look through the bars. I can't see anything and don't know what's causing the racket. I call out loudly, "What's the matter?"

"A girl's having a fit in her cell—bang your door!"

I know it's Victoria from the Belmont Home. She's isolated at the far end of the corridor but the girl in the nearby cell can hear her.

Finding that a space exists between the door and the padlocked chair, I firmly grasp the bars of my door. Using all my weight, I yank them back and forth, creating as much din as possible. Finally we hear the metallic sound of the many keys a matron carries. I can see her through the bars, running past my cell looking confused, wondering which way to turn. The girls call out, directing her to the furthest cell. I can hear the rattle of keys as the matron searches for the right one, then the grating of the door being unlocked.

Victoria's epileptic seizures happen often—she can't take being in the Mercer. Despite the excitement, the noise, and light, I'm sound asleep within minutes.

*S*ince our arrival we've been conditioned to obey orders without delay. We expect nothing from the matrons. We don't know it's a violation of the rules for them to be friendly.

As time and responsibility rest heavily on a matron, her tone of voice is always strident. I never hear a girl say she has preference for one matron over another.

Talking time in our ward after supper is short—about half an hour, depending, I suppose, on how busy the matron is. The women feel reluctant to leave off their conversations and be locked in. Evening in the cell is long and silent. The book usually handed out each fortnight is soon read. A matron passes by our cells with a cart full of storybooks. Through the bars she receives the previous book and hands out another, asking, "Have you read this one?" I say no and accept it.

Because there are no cells facing us, we can't see one another nor can we tell when a matron is about. A girl seldom calls out to another from her cell. It's not allowed and a matron might hear us. No one knows what would happen and we are too scared to find out.

⌒

J never become used to my cell. Each morning I open my eyes and feel despair. Drab grey and hard surfaces have replaced the colour and texture of former surroundings. Barred windows and cells are constant reminders that all freedom of movement is constricted. But I was not born in captivity.

I don't think about my fiancée anymore; my loyalties have dissolved in a sea of turmoil. I am still in shock. I will never think of sexuality nor even menstruate when the time comes. All my thoughts are directed toward the immediacy of my situation and my vulnerability, such as lack of access to my physical needs. My environment has taken over my entire being—there is no spirituality, no romance, only pragmatism. My heavy body has separated me from others. I feel like an animal that needs reprieve from suffering.

No one ever told me that I'm carrying a human being inside me and I don't acknowledge its existence. There's a silent conspiracy to undermine that reality since I have antagonized the state by my monstrous behaviour.

*C*HAPTER 3

*M*y mother says, "Sit down and I'll tell your fortune."
She's wearing a bright bandanna around her head. It's her own style. She believes she's the child of gypsies who left her with her English parents. She deals out every thirteenth card, talking all the while. She never asks questions because to each card she has given a meaning. The six of clubs means money and the seven of diamonds deals with financial matters, favourable or not depending on whether they're accompanied with hearts or spades. Spades of course are the bad cards and she will advise a client to be cautious.

"The future must always offer hope or they won't come back," she says. Anyhow, it's not her way to discourage anyone. Most clients are middle-aged women. Many repeat visitors speak confidentially to her. "I tell them, 'Don't ask for anything until you've given your husband a good meal and he's in good humour.'"

When they're gone she says, "Why don't they leave? —Don't want to lose a free meal ticket!"

My mother gains my attention by telling my fortune. Her flow of words ceases only when she has counted and dealt out every thirteenth card until thirteen cards lie in a row. She then summarizes the results. We speculate on the outcome but the predictions are vague. She's told my fortune a number of times before and it now fails to hold our attention for long. I'm her confidante and this is a preliminary ritual for her reminiscing that always follows. She's dipping into her memory for her most vivid experiences. Most of these concern her ex-husband, my father. The full storm of her feelings, her humiliation, must be told over and over again.

"The doctor said I would go into consumption if I continued the way I was going. It was decided I should go to England with your grandmother. On the boat I learned to dance the tango and smoke."

She rises, raises her arms, and demonstrates the long rhythmic steps.

"Your grandmother said 'I'm going to tell your husband when we get back.'"

"We were on the deck and I said, 'Come one step closer and I'll throw you overboard.'"

"Your father used to call me 'dumb Dora.' When I got back I went into his restaurant with my bobbed hair, sat down, and blew smoke into his face and laughed."

But soon exhilaration is replaced by pain and humiliation. My father's infidelity was established by the court at the divorce hearing. And his crimes continue.

"He hadn't sent me my alimony and when your brother got sick he came up to Quebec City to take my children away from me." "Fifty dollars a month!" She sneers. "It's the same amount the government gives to a widow with two children—not what a businessman should pay. Your father had a disease, that's why he wasn't sleeping with me."

My mother refuses to consider she wasn't desirable to my father, or to any man for that matter. She dreams out loud and I never know when her intentions are wishful thinking. Her promises are sometimes real enough, or they may fade away. A planned evening out may result in "I think I'll lie down." A change in direction is rationalized by "I always go by my feelings."

"Your father pushed me downstairs."

She says it plaintively like it's too extreme to be believed. I feel a pang of guilt. I can't tell her I was standing at the bottom of the long straight stairway looking up at the disturbance. In childish wonder I watched. My father was emerging from the open door of a bedroom near the top of the stairs and my mother was screaming at him and trying to hit him with a hairbrush. My father kept trying to grab it from the hand of her extended arm, his body easing her dangerously to the edge of the steps. She fell down the stairs backwards, somersaulting to the bottom where she lay crumpled and sobbing. I can't admit witnessing the scene. I didn't see my father push her, but not to agree with my mother would suggest disloyalty. I respect my father because his actions coincide with his words. I resent my mother for engaging in fantasy and self-praise.

My mother divorced my father for adultery in New Brunswick in 1928 when I was eight years old and my brother was ten. She now runs a rooming house and tea room on Church Street in Toronto across from the Maple Leaf Gardens. A sign in the window reads *Madam Alice*

Teacup Reading. Why Worry? When I was sixteen I would sometimes serve tea to her patrons.

My mother met my father during World War I, when he owned an ice cream parlour and candy store called the Palm Gardens at the corner of Union and Cobourg Streets in Saint John, New Brunswick. My mother, a farm girl working as a maid in the city, married my father despite the prejudice against South European foreigners. They lived upstairs over the store. Later, she borrowed money from her relatives and helped my father, together with a partner, buy a building in a central location across from King's Square. There they set up a high-class restaurant called the Paradise where my mother's services were no longer needed so she embarked on a social life of little interest to my father. Having worked in my father's ice cream parlour as cashier and candy maker for ten years, she received no wages. There's not a day passes that she doesn't relate the terrible things she would like to do to my father. She's sure her mystic powers will lead him to disaster.

—

This afternoon finds my mother in the yard brushing down mattresses with kerosene to kill the bedbugs. Roy is in the basement building a trailer for her. My mother says, "You know, Roy used to work for the post office and he was a Mason." I know that belonging to a fellowship like the Masons is highly regarded.

"Roy's good with his hands," she says.

Roy comes up from the basement and goes out. I can see he's been drinking. My mother lets him keep the money that he gets from parking the cars of the Maple Leaf Gardens hockey fans in our backyard. Roy is a good-natured Irishman but he goes on periodical drinking binges. There will be a fight but my mother can't put him out until the trailer is finished. Unless all caution is thrown to the winds when she loses her temper. "I took all the beer out of the ice box and threw it in the yard," she says defiantly.

Still, it is in my mother's nature to be forgiving. Just as she forgives Roy for his drunken behaviour, she forgives others. "Take your notice and be out of here at the end of the month," she hollers to the drunken elderly pensioners on the third floor who fight and disturb the peace each payday. The following morning the man's wife comes round soliciting my mother's sympathy.

My mother lets them stay.

—

J hear the muted ring of the doorbell. The door is opened and it now stands ajar. A neatly dressed slender woman is standing there looking slightly annoyed. She has twisted the bell to get attention. She asks for Mrs. Cottrell. I immediately call to my mother and tell her.

The woman says, "I went upstairs and knocked on Mrs. Cottrell's door but there's no answer." I realize she's been here before and knows which door to knock on.

My mother says, "Mrs. Cottrell just went out to the store."

There's nowhere to wait and nothing further is said but my mother knows she'll be back.

"She's from the Welfare," my mother tells me. "They're checking up. I'll have to warn Mrs. Cottrell to come home right away."

My mother picks up the phone. Within fifteen minutes Mrs. Cottrell arrives all out of breath. Although no one is listening my mother whispers, "She hasn't come back yet." There are quick conspiratorial exchanges and Mrs. Cottrell scurries upstairs. Mrs. Cottrell has stealthily obtained a day job doing housework to supplement her meager allowance. The income will provide her with a little cash, unlike welfare which provides only vouchers.

"A person can be cut off welfare if they find so much as an empty beer bottle in a room," my mother advises.

Another welfare recipient lives in our basement. A door from the hall leads down to the below-ground basement with its buckled cement floor. Grimy half-windows divided into quarter panes provide insufficient light and an electric light bulb burns constantly in the storage room where a woman and her four-year-old daughter live. The wire to an electric hot plate hangs from the double socket of the light bulb. Access to water is from the taps over the large concrete tubs. Our washing machine stands nearby. The woman gives me a welfare chit and asks me to go to the store. I feel terribly embarrassed presenting the ticket to the grocer for a bottle of milk. It's a disgrace to be on welfare.

Mr. Saunders, a tall lanky man, lives in a room on the third floor with his wife and two children next door to the pensioners.

"Tomorrow," my mother says, "I'm taking Mr. Saunders out to sell vacuum cleaners—we'll go to houses on the outskirts of the city." After hoisting the vacuum cleaners for demonstration purposes into the car, she grabs the banister, climbs a few stairs, and calls out loudly, "Mr. Saunders, I'm ready to go!"

A woman who tells my mother her troubles buys a vacuum cleaner. "You have to sell yourself first," my mother says.

Last weekend she assisted a Native Canadian in his medicine show. "I held a cigarette in my mouth and he cut it off with a whip," she tells me. The Depression has made everyone resourceful.

I'm eating Laura Secord chocolates out of their second largest box. They were bought by my mother's admirer, a farmer who visits occasionally. My mother and this man who is wearing a suit sit demurely in the sitting room and talk. Why doesn't she marry someone like that? She met him through a newspaper ad she'd inserted. She would never dream of answering an ad. "Let them come to me," she says. Aside from playing up a good figure she makes no attempt to lure the opposite sex. She dabs on a little powder and rouge and it lasts all day. She spends no time on clothing. She's convinced that every man is attracted to her personality. These days our icebox is packed with wieners, sausages, and meat. She doesn't explain why but I know it has something to do with white-haired Mr. Groten who has a butcher shop. My mother says, "When I was reading Mrs. Groten's teacup she asked me if her husband would return to her. I said, 'Yes, I see him coming back to you but he'll be broke.'"

She advises, "Hold onto the bone and the dog will follow."

My mother sleeps on the first floor in a large bedroom. The door is seldom open but a couple of times when it was, I saw a pulled-out chesterfield bed and the untidiness of a place that doesn't need attention. I don't know where Roy sleeps and I never ask. I don't breach my mother's privacy nor question her ways.

There's good humour and anticipation all day long when Miss Halliday takes my mother out for supper at the Royal York Hotel. "Miss Halliday is waiting for her aunt to die so she can get her money," my mother says. "Her aunt is sick and I have to look in the teacup to see how long she'll last. I'd better see her getting worse or it will never do."

It's quiet in our house when my mother goes out. Except for the occasional roomer wanting her attention, there are no social calls. My brother can be heard playing his violin in his room on the second floor. He chastises my mother, "Why wasn't I taught the violin when I was young?"

"You didn't want to practise, you wanted to go out and play."

"Why didn't you beat me?" he persists.

We have a piano but my mother doesn't play anymore. She has a soprano voice and played the piano before the divorce. On rare occasions she sings when we have company.

My brother has a brace with steel rods so he can stand up. My mother went to a government office to get help to buy the brace but they wouldn't pay for it. My mother said, "The man behind me offered to pay."

It was decided that my brother should take an art course instead of business. "Your brother is good at drawing ships," she says. I know that he uses a ruler but my opinion would be demeaned. I don't say anything. He makes good marks in academic subjects but does poorly in art.

Through a crippled children's fund supported by the Shriners, my mother is able to get my brother a trip on a freighter for two weeks. It's a highlight for all of us. Later, during the war, my brother would get an office job. When he made a minor criticism, he was told, "You're lucky to have a job." He never went back.

I don't feel my brother's pain, his terrible isolation and dependency. He's always in his room, never goes anywhere. Some people will see him on the street on crutches and shake their heads in sympathy. My brother is proud and hates to be demeaned. Before the divorce he always came first on his report card in school.

Returning home from the Royal York, my mother says, "I told Miss Halliday, 'Get your money out of the bank and be ready to go. It won't be long now.'"

—

$\mathcal{M}$iss Halliday is visiting in the tearoom. She's back from attending her aunt's funeral.

My mother is going to Lindsay with the trailer to read teacups. It's one of the small towns she visits. A couple of months ago she went to Barrie. It's a good idea, she says, not to go to the same place too often. She'll park the trailer and put out a teacup-reading sign. She has now taken over the rooming house next door as well. She says, "I want you to take care of the houses until I get back." She drives off, hauling the small trailer she will sleep in that Roy built. She'll be back in a couple of days, depending on business.

It's about two in the morning when a roomer from the second rooming house tells me there's a noise. A small unshaven elderly pensioner is in bed with a half-dressed woman and there are two men on the floor. They're all drunk and singing loudly.

"I'll give you just five minutes to get out!" I say firmly to the unwanted guests. I must act quickly lest the police come and declare the place a disorderly house—no one will be allowed to have liquor on the premises for a year and my mother will have to pay a fine. Only the other night the police converged on several houses in the area and arrested a number of people for breach of the Liquor Control Act. Nobody pays any attention to me so I call the police. They take everybody away in the paddy wagon except the pensioner. The police ask, "How old are you?"

"Seventeen," I say. I explain my mother is away.

"Could you give me the names and occupations of all the tenants?"

I supply them as best I can.

"Doesn't anyone in these houses work?"

When my mother returns she doesn't say whether I did right or wrong but I know police attention is undesirable. She would have handled the situation on her own, picked up the woman and men, and thrown them out. She's very strict about women bringing strange men into their rooms. "Out they go!" she says. "I don't care what they do outside."

She laughs and tells me, "When I asked Cherie for her rent—she opened the door and said, 'I'm sorry mum—I couldn't make any money this week 'cause I have my monthly.'"

—

I'm sleeping in an empty room when my mother calls to me to unlock the door. I hurry to get out of bed and let her in. She turns the key in the lock and says, "Frank is looking for me, don't say I'm here." Frank is my mother's new boyfriend. He's Italian and makes wonderful meals when he comes over.

He knocks on the door and calls out, "Is your mother there?"

"No, she's not here," I say. I can hear him outside the door, unwilling to leave.

My mother says, "Why do I have to be afraid of him?"

She opens the door and Frank makes a lunge towards her but she ducks. She starts hollering, "What do you mean barging in here? Who do you think you are?"

Frank's rage is directed elsewhere. He goes looking for Roy and finds him sleeping in the trailer in the backyard. I look out the window to see Frank chasing Roy who is in his drawers running around the adjacent parking lot.

———

Che only part of our house that looks nice is the tearoom. It has large front windows and lace curtains, small round tables with checkered red and white tablecloths, and uncracked decorative linoleum on the floor. The worn linoleum in the kitchen and hallways is washed with a mop that never gets into the corners. There's a metal tea-leaf catcher in the corner of the kitchen sink which has damaged and stained the enamel. Nearby is a bar of yellow lye soap for washing dishes. For this purpose, we heat water in the kettle on the gas stove. There's no water in the rooms and only the two on the top floor have two-burner gas jets for cooking. There's one bathroom on the second floor for all of us. When a tenant wants hot water for a bath, my mother goes down to the basement and lights the gas jet under the hot water boiler.

Due to the expense, it's turned off after a few minutes. Occasionally the wrong person goes into the bathroom and uses up all the hot water.

My mother comes into the kitchen and screams at me. "Why didn't you put the potatoes on?"

She bites her hand in fury as I race towards the potato sack. She likes boiled potatoes. We have them at every meal and often we open a can of pork and beans to go with them. But there's always a roast on Sunday—it's a tradition from way back.

I'm sent upstairs to sweep the carpet in Mr Petroni's room. It's covered with cigarette butts. Mr. Petroni, a small middle-aged man with a lump on the side of his nose, sits in a rocking chair and I sweep around him. For some reason he always calls me Betty. He makes a sudden movement and I scratch his face. He's upset and I feel I made a mistake. He asks, "Betty! Why did you do that?"

I don't know why but I don't apologize.

It seems we can never get this house clean. The bedbugs follow us from one place to the next. Perhaps because my mother comes from the country she's not afraid of bugs. In Quebec City when I was in bed behind a screen, I called out, "There's a bedbug climbing up the wall."

My mother said, "Keep quiet and go to sleep!"

Since I returned to her home from my father's place, sixteen years old and all grown up, she no longer flies off the handle. She measures female worth by attractiveness to men. My morose attitude is gone and I no longer resent her. I didn't tell her that her boyfriend was making overtures to me in the kitchen when she was reading teacups in the front room. Rather, I left home and hitchhiked to Montreal. When I walked into a Greek restaurant there, my father's name insured my security, and I was transported to New Brunswick. I was fifteen then and lived with my father for a year and a half. I'm actually not one for taking chances, possibly due to my mother's stories of her narrow escapes.

My father said, "You're crazy!"

I didn't tell him my reason for hitchhiking. It would have added more grist to the mill. I'd be tainted with my mother's failings.

My father adroitly transfers guilt for the divorce onto my mother. She was wild—went dancing every night and shamed him by bringing us children into the restaurant without washing our hands and face. It's said repeatedly. My mother's actions since the divorce, her occupation as teacup reader, confirm her as an object of ridicule.

He always says she went dancing when I know she was playing cards. I can remember the card tables set up when she entertained at our house, the silver tea set and the glass-topped tea wagon. I would peek at the guests through the top of the banister. In the morning I would feast on the leftovers—trimmed little sandwiches and patty pans filled with fruit in the shape of little baskets that my mother made.

—

*M*y father's family lives in an apartment on the third floor over the restaurant. His partner's family and a dentist's office are on the second floor. My father and his partner own the brick building on Charlotte Street. This apartment with its shiny hardwood floors, thick rug, polished furniture, and hot water contrasts with my mother's shabby rooming house. The regular routine at my father's house satisfies my need for security.

It's noon when I leave school and go to the restaurant for dinner. I pass the long gleaming soda fountain on the right, the display cases of chocolates and cash register on the left, and walk up an aisle to an empty booth. I always take my meals alone.

The canaries can be heard singing in their three individual cages hanging from the ceiling. They're brought down every morning by one of the waitresses. The cages are cleaned and replenished with seed and water and hoisted up again. There are two ornate water fountains between the aisles.

I can order anything except the most expensive items on the menu. My father eats specially prepared Greek dishes with his wife upstairs in the apartment. On festive occasions I'm invited to join them.

After school I work as a cashier in my father's theatre. There's no communication with family to speak of. My father is always busy. I barely notice, however, because I'm absorbed in the movies. I watch double features at the theatre where I work and, as a theatre employee, I have unlimited access to two other theatres in town.

Yet sometimes when no one's at home I sit sobbing in the kitchen. I don't quite understand why. I tell my father I'm quitting school. Each province has its own curriculum and I was put back two years because of moving around. My breast size has enlarged and I'm self-conscious among my classmates. There are no older students in class. Students who fail are likely to come from a poorer class and will drop out and go to work before reaching high school.

My father puts me in the kitchen of the restaurant washing dishes and large pots for one day. Then he promotes me to the soda fountain where I make salads, sandwiches, and sundaes. I'm not loyal to my father. I steal cigarettes from his store, though I would never steal from my mother.

—

*W*hatever our differences, my mother and I share the illicit secrets which have sustained us as a family. In Quebec City, she said, "Don't come home after school today—I'll meet you." When we meet she says, "We had a fire." She's finally getting the insurance money for the furniture and we're driving to Ontario. I know she was in a tough spot. Emile, her French-Canadian boyfriend, leased the rooming house in his own name and could put us out anytime; my mother can't read French. My brother is thirteen years old and has just been released from hospital, his legs paralyzed from infantile paralysis. I'm eleven. First, we visit the shrine at Ste. Anne de Beaupré and climb the high steps on our knees, hoping for a miracle that will cure my brother. We can see crutches that have been left behind by those who have been healed. My mother hangs a St. Joseph's medal over the front window of the car for good luck. Before leaving Quebec, my mother buys a large quantity of salted peanuts, which we put into small bags. She also purchases a dozen aluminum pans from the five and dime store.

—

*W*e're in a small town in Quebec and Emile has gotten drunk. We drive off, leaving our male assistant behind—a man to carry my brother to the bathroom. The doctor had told my mother, "He will never get out of a chair."

We urge our mother to keep going.

The road we take leads through the hinterlands of Quebec and we have no difficulty in exchanging pans for meals with poor French Canadians. We sell the bags of peanuts to the owners of small country grocery stores. We sleep on cedar boughs to keep the ants away. A little brandy in our coffee keeps us well. As we pass through Ontario we encounter a large crowd, including many in wheelchairs, along the road and in a treed area behind a low open fence. The people must be believers in the famous Dr. Locke's curative powers and they're lined up waiting for his attention. We watch him from outside the fence while he makes quick twists to the feet of patients and puts bills into his pocket.

A farmer refuses to let us pitch our tent in his field so we set up our tent on the shores of Lake Ontario. My mother stays awake all night afraid the tide will come in—there's a huge tide in New Brunswick because it's on the sea.

CHAPTER 4

*T*he alienation of my father's home is in contrast to my mother's where, despite its physical drawbacks, I have the feeling of belonging. My interests in Saint John were outside, in my father's theatre where I worked as cashier after school. Sometimes we had a vaudeville act.

One performance was "The Great Santini," a slender young man in a tuxedo with two pretty girls in evening gowns. He claimed to have psychic powers and would answer questions from the audience. The theatre assistant told me he had a small microphone under his collar and could hear remarks from the audience. He hypnotized one of his assistants and put her into a store window. I saw her outstretched on her back, sleeping on a bed. Later I was told that the window shattered because of the large crowd trying to see. At the box office I was inundated with calls from women wanting to make an appointment with the Great Santini.

Another act was the Siamese twins from the Philippines who were joined at the waist. They came with their wives who we were told were sisters. The twins rode a specially constructed bicycle around the stage.

Now in my mother's home I have retained these interests. I go alone to the Casino, a vaudeville show on Queen Street in Toronto, with comedy acts, dancing, and striptease. The girls who do the striptease remove their clothes gracefully and always leave on a brassiere and a cover over their private parts. This day, two Chinese men and their girlfriends are sitting in front of me. The women who have French accents are wearing fur coats. Their companions could be business-men. They may have come down from Montreal, I think. I envy their well-being and enjoyment.

A religious old Ukrainian man who lives on the second floor takes me to his church. We go to Queen and Soho Streets. A sign over the door says *Pentecostal*. Inside a few people are sitting on hard wooden chairs. A white preacher standing up front is speaking. "Praise the Lord!" he exclaims repeatedly. One woman answers, "Amen!" Another man is moving in an agitated manner and speaking strangely. My friend says he's talking in tongues.

My mother's fortune-telling invites personal confessions. One woman admits to being a streetwalker to support her daughter who is in boarding school.

—

I'm in a Chinese restaurant with my mother, Linda, and a quiet French-Canadian girl, sitting at a round table with a white cotton tablecloth. We've chosen a table near the front where a half curtain stretched across the bottom of the window affords a certain privacy from pedestrians. Several Chinese waiters wearing white shirts and ties are serving customers at the many tables.

Linda looks Spanish with straight black hair drawn back from her forehead. Her eyebrows are pencilled in. My mother says she's hiding out from the police, though she doesn't say why. Linda looks composed like an unruffled duchess. The presence of this attractive and clandestine woman in our midst lends excitement. My mother always sympathizes with the poor, the welfare recipients, and the escapees from bureaucracy.

We've had a drink somewhere and are happy. This social gathering outside our home is unusual for my mother and me. A handsome Chinese waiter is serving us. I drop my fork—he picks it up. Carelessly, I drop it again. He retrieves it a second time. We laugh. The waiter laughs and says, "How about a date?"

I answer, "All right."

This adds to the hilarity. I tell him I'll meet him at the restaurant the following day. Everybody thinks we're kidding. Except us.

—

*T*here had been a couple of boys in Saint John who had shown interest in me. I liked the attention but that was all. One boy asked me to marry him. I told him I was too young. But even the most attractive boy couldn't have persuaded me to live on my father's turf. Saint John was the place where my father and his wife lived in their quiet contented way. It was both the symbol of how and the place where my mother had become the outsider. Her lifestyle had been my example. I watched films that never showed families but only the immediacy of romance and the mystery of the unknown.

When I was working behind the soda fountain, there was a fellow who came regularly into the restaurant. When he persisted in asking me out, I asked a waitress I trusted about him. "He's OK as far as I know but he's too old for you. He must be twenty-seven or twenty-eight." I was sixteen.

The man was a chemist in a lab of some kind. I went out with him. After we'd driven around for a while, he parked in a remote place and began to make sexual overtures. I told him I'd never been with anyone before. "Well, I'm going to find out!" he said. My physical resistance was easily overcome by his athletic strength. Afterwards he said, "Just to show that I believe you, I'm not going back to my lab to clean up."

I went to a dance although my father forbade it and came home in the early hours of the morning. I had been drinking. It happened some days after the rape, which I didn't tell anyone about. That same day my father packed me off by train to my mother in Toronto. He placed me in the care of a Greek fellow who was going in that direction on his way to Boston.

---

*N*ow there is no status to uphold, no bonds to be severed as I embark on a culturally unpopular course. I know that going out with a Chinese man is socially unacceptable. There may be disapproving looks from passersby but I don't care. It's the first time I look forward with such eagerness to a date. I thought we might go to a show but instead he leads me to his quarters. I believe I'm completely safe because the Chinese are not generally considered aggressive.

My new friend guides me up the stairs of a rather ancient house to his isolated room on the third floor. He hangs up my coat, removes my shoes, and puts my feet into his slippers. Removing his own shoes, he remains with his socks on. He pours vermouth into two tiny whiskey glasses and we sip it slowly. We smoke cigarettes and talk.

"My name is Harry Yip," he says.

"Mine is Velma."

"Where do you live?" he asks.

"With my mother on Church Street."

He smiles.

He shows me an official document of his entry into Canada with the name "Yip Kum Kuey" and points to a picture. "That's me," he jokes.

Harry is fourteen years old in the photograph and looking solemnly ahead. He's at least ten years older than I am. I'm seventeen.

"Do you have any family in China?"

"I have a mother and a sister," he says hesitantly.

"Do you write to them?"

"No, I don't know where they are. I never go back to China."

I don't see any Chinese newspapers about. Perhaps he never learned to read Chinese.

"I taught myself to read and write English," he says as if he's read my mind.

I tell him about my mother, that she's divorced. He's amused and interested to learn that my mother is a fortune-teller.

"Are there other people living in this house? It's so quiet."

"Other people live here but they're working," he says.

I remark on his looks. He shrugs his shoulder apologetically. "Sometimes a customer says, 'How come you're so good-looking for a Chinese?'" He stands up, indicating he has to return to work.

"Do you mind if I kiss you?"

"No," I answer.

He places a light kiss on my lips.

―

The house is on Walton Street. It's a few blocks from Chinatown and just west of Yonge Street where the restaurants are located. I ascend the wooden steps of the old turreted brick building. It's similar to others on the street. The front door is unlocked. There's no bell. He must have already arrived and is expecting me. I climb the well-worn steps, past the second floor landing where the bathroom is located. A window facing north at the top of the stairs provides light. A banister curves round. His door is the first one on the third floor.

There's also another door but I don't know if anyone lives there. The house is silent as it was during my previous visit.

He opens the door immediately at my knock but I know he's been listening for my footsteps on the stairs. He welcomes me with smiles. The soft aroma of incense greets me as I ascend the third landing. This is my second visit and our ritual is the same. Fresh fruit is in the bowl on the emerald green linoleum that has been cut and glued onto the table, and he is again pouring vermouth for me into a tiny glass, a thimble. We may have a second drink, but no more.

Water is boiling in a kettle over the flames of a two-burner gas element. He must have filled the kettle from the downstairs tap in the bathroom before my arrival. Beneath the cabinet on which the gas plate rests are shelves for pots and dishes. He pushes aside the cotton cloth hiding the shelves and retrieves cups and a teapot. He's making English tea. Out of the punctured holes of a can of Eagle Brand condensed milk, he removes matchsticks and allows the sweet syrupy liquid to ooze slowly into my cup of hot brew. Chinese biscuits that taste like shortbread are arranged on a plate.

The initial stage of our romance has been secured. I've proven my reliability by returning, and he has proven his by being here. Relaxed, I look at my surroundings.

The room isn't large but it's sufficient. The walls are unevenly beige. Coats and pressed pants are visible, hanging from a built-in clothes closet. The room is in the back of the building and from the window can be seen the roofs of other houses, some tall enough to shade the room from excessive light. There are drapes and a green blind that can be pulled down.

Although it's summer the room is cool. A three-quarter size bed with a soft green bedspread rests beside the wall. Covering the linoleum in front of the bed is a small rug. An alarm clock rests on a flowered centrepiece on a dresser. There's no radio.

My friend has removed his tie and placed it on the walnut dresser. His starched white shirt is open at the neck and I glimpse his white undershirt. He has pushed up his shirt cuffs and I observe he's wearing what appears to be an expensive watch with a gold band. On his finger is a gold ring with a black stone.

During my previous visit I had worn his slippers while he sat with his stocking feet on the cold linoleum. This time, with a dramatic gesture, he removes my shoes and produces a pretty pair of blue hand-embroidered slippers that he gently eases onto my feet. He's pleased with my response.

"How did you know my size?"

He doesn't answer but I realize he was noting my size during my previous visit.

"I'll get some keys made so you can come any time," he says.

$\sim$

$\mathcal{H}$arry and I are spending our first night together. He kisses me tenderly and goes to sleep.

I'm impressed by his respect, his discipline. I keep coming back here. I idle my time away in his room. Gradually I remove myself from my mother's sphere, the bedbugs, her alcoholic boyfriend, the chaos, and my brother's condescending behaviour.

Even before my parents' divorce and before his illness, I resented my brother. He was the leader. At my birthday party my friends left and followed him. My mother dotes on him.

My mother was eight years old when she came to Canada with her English parents from England. Most of the troops going overseas during World War I to fight for the British Empire were British or Canadians of British heritage. Anglo-Saxon superiority was ingrained in the British loyalist community of Saint John and immigrants from southern Europe were looked down on. My mother had married beneath the accepted standards of the community and her pregnancy further estranged her. Attempts to ingratiate herself with the few Greek women in the city were hardly successful. Among her own nationality she hadn't the sophistication to resist the barbs cast at her, nor could she hide, escape, nor argue with her critics. As a lone defender in her isolated situation she said, "When I married your father, a friend said I'd have a black baby. When your brother had fair hair and blue eyes, I was so proud pushing the baby carriage along the street."

I have dark brown hair and dark eyes. I'm often taken for French.

"Why do you let her go out with an Oriental?" my brother demands angrily.

"Mind your own business," my mother replies, then asks me "Why don't you spend more time at home?"

"Tomorrow for sure," I say.

$\sim$

$\mathcal{I}$t's evening and I'm waiting for my boyfriend to finish work. I pour Chinese tea into a miniature bowl from a blue thermos left on the table. Harry's clothes are neatly hung in his wardrobe and I pass my hand over his suits, jackets, ties, and bathrobe and inhale the sweet scent of starched shirts folded in his dresser drawer, fresh from a Chinese laundry. We'll eat when he arrives. I don't know how to cook. Anyway, I won't eat without him.

He makes creamy custard. He's a master of fine food. He boils chicken with ginger or fries beef with Chinese mushrooms and greens and serves it with steamed rice. Sometimes we have barbequed duck or roast chicken that he buys in Chinatown. In the morning he fries bananas in an omelette with bacon. Almond cakes, oranges, apples, and grapes are left on the table for me to nibble on. During a Chinese festival he buys mooncakes that are delicious.

I've changed into my pyjamas and am wearing his bathrobe when he comes in. He puts on his slippers before removing his jacket and commences steaming some buns filled with pork and vegetables. As he works I admire his strong sure hands, his fingernails trimly filed, his deft movements as each mundane task assumes the utmost importance.

He has an upright build, symmetrical, not wide-shouldered, tall but not too tall. His short black hair is groomed with a touch of ointment on his fingertips skimmed from a small ornate Chinese jar. It's brushed straight back, smooth, and shiny. He has a wide forehead and a sensitive narrow face. Heavy brows cover flashing dark eyes over chiselled high cheekbones. His feelings are clearly etched as he speaks and he projects optimism. He smiles easily.

"Were you busy tonight?" I ask.

"Not so busy. Some customers like to joke around," he says, looking amused.

I imagine him bantering with them as he did with me that first day we met. He continues. "Some lofan (white men) come in late—they don't want to leave—drink too much." He frowns and shakes his head.

He has brought home several pairs of sample shoes, removes my slippers, and tries them on my small feet. We agree on the pair I keep. He determines my style, but I like the attention. It is such a contrast to my mother who shrank my good dress in the washing machine.

Harry produces a bottle of orange gin. It's a surprise, a celebration for no particular reason.

"It's sweet," I say.

We laugh.

We go to bed and hold each other close. I want him with his smooth arms, his slender hands, and almost thin build. I trace my fingers over his high cheekbones, his slightly aquiline nose. I pass my hand over his almost hairless chest. He closes his eyes. His curved lids and dark eye-lashes beguile me.

There's a certain modesty in the way we touch each other's body. We bend to each other's thoughts; there's no disagreement.

Yet there's a firmness about him, an expectation of certain standards. He says, "You should hang up your coat." I'm unhurt by criticism. I don't want to be careless, to follow the disruptive life I've known.

I finger his strong black hair. It has the faint odour of smoke. I know it's from the kitchen where he works. I think of the kitchen in my father's restaurant with the waitresses calling out orders to the irate Greek chef.

Harry is working a split shift with long hours just as I had done behind the soda fountain: time off in the afternoon then back to work for supper and the evening, but he works even longer hours and has no days off.

Our lovemaking is not lengthy but we love each other and are content.

On occasion, in the early hours before morning when he finishes work, we walk towards Chinatown. It's summer. The sky is filled with stars and a warm breeze bathes my skin. I feel enraptured. He walks erect, looking straight ahead, not turning to speak, but I can see an amiable curl to his lips. Words are unnecessary.

He wears tinted glasses—heaven knows why—which adds to his shadowy appearance. His fedora hat is slanted at an angle. He's my gangster, just like in the movies. He's my George Raft, my Humphrey Bogart. I'm thrilled by heroes—self-made men with guns and ingenuity. There's an element of mystery about Harry that bewitches me. I'm leaving the chaotic world of my mother and the alienated society of my father. I'm finding love, peace, security.

He takes me up the rickety steps of a restaurant in Chinatown. The place is utilitarian. Chinese men are eating at tables covered with white oilcloth but the food is good. There are no white people here. Harry exchanges greetings with the waiter in Chinese. Everyone can see how happy we are. Everyone wants a girlfriend.

—

There are sounds, some movement on the second floor, quick tapping steps. I go downstairs to the bathroom to find the door of a room slightly open. A girl comes out and says, "Hello. I'm staying with Joe Wah. I'm from Barrie."

"You're from Barrie?" I ask.

"Yeah, I was going 'round with a Chinese guy there who works in a restaurant but we broke up."

"Did you work there too?"

"No, of course not," she laughs. "White girls aren't allowed to work in Chinese places. It's the law."

"How old are you?" I ask.

"Sixteen."

"I'm seventeen," I say.

"My name is Ellen," she offers. I'm struck by her attractiveness.

"I once won a beauty contest," she says.

In a few days she knocks on Harry's door. "I finally got you in. Harry told me you were at your mother's. I'm going to stay with Jimmy Chen—he's part owner of a restaurant." She writes down the address. "You can come and see me."

I arrive at the Elm Street address and knock on the door. It's easy to recognize Chinese houses. Bachelor houses don't have polished windows and tidy curtains.

I'm nervous—I could be pegged as a girl looking for "business" standing there. The downstairs window doesn't look too bad. Someone quickly brushes open the curtains and I'm let in. A Caucasian male is suspect. He could push his way in. Ellen is in Jimmy Chen's flat on the first floor. The rooms upstairs are rented to Chinese farmers who work on large farms outside the city.

"They're out most of the time," says Ellen.

A French-Canadian woman with a baby is visiting. The baby has Chinese features. When the woman talks to the baby in Chinese, I comment on her ability.

"I just picked it up," she says.

French Canadians are so resourceful, I think. The woman is incensed over a recent incident. "When I was crossing Elizabeth Street, somebody called out, 'Look at that white woman with the Chinky baby.'"

I share her anger. I'm curious about the baby's father but feel afraid to ask. Is she living with him or someone else? She wants to explain. She knows we're sympathetic.

"I told Ken, the baby's father, I'm not marrying a Chinese. What if I have to get a job? How will I get one with a Chinese name? Then too, you can lose your citizenship if you marry a foreigner."

I feel her remarks are disloyal. If Harry had leprosy I'd go into segregation behind barbed wire with him.

"How do you like living here?" I ask Ellen.

"Fine," she says. "Jimmy had another girl living with him before. He said he kicked her out for running around."

Later, I ask Harry, "Does Jimmy Chen have a wife in China?"

"I think so."

"Ellen says he told her he didn't have a wife in China but she found a picture."

"I don't know," he says. "I don't know him very well."

"Do you have a wife in China?"

"No, I tell you—I never go back to China!" I hear him talking in Chinese to Joe Wah downstairs and hear Ellen's name.

"What did he say about Ellen?" I ask.

"He says she's a prostitute."

"Why?" I ask. "Because she doesn't want him? I wouldn't want him either." He smiles.

—

*M*y head hurts. The noise of the traffic is painful and I can barely make it to Harry's room. I lie unmoving on the green woven bedspread and wait for the sound of his key in the lock. I remain this way, never looking at the clock. Time is never the enemy. My lover never says, "Why didn't you come?" Neither do I question his whereabouts. Our times together are unplanned, spontaneous. He prefers to see my reaction when he says, "Let's go to Chinatown to eat!" Or, "See what I've got..."

Tonight after work he went to a restaurant in Chinatown and bought some barbequed duck. It's cut in pieces. He cooks some rice. I tell him, "My mother says my nerves are bad. I should go and stay with my grandmother in Saint John for a rest."

"Your grandmother?" he enquires. "I didn't know you had a grandmother."

"I would go for a month," I say.

He rubs some Tiger Balm on the temples of my forehead to ease the pain. He respects family ties.

"A rest would be good for you," he says.

"You can write to me," I say.

—

My father visits me at my grandmother's house in Saint John. Immediately my loyalty to my boyfriend conflicts with my father's smug opinions. My head aches and I cry easily.

"What's wrong with you?" my father demands. To my father, emotion is a sign of weakness. "When there's no money to pay the bills, love flies out the window," he asserts.

General Delivery at the post office hands over my mail. Harry sends me his picture. We'll marry when I return.

—

Jt's now the spring of 1939 and Easter has barely passed when I return to Toronto. My fiancé and I have been in love for over a year. This time, for the first time after visiting my father, I'm not returning to my mother's home. I am eloping. But what a disappointment! Our marriage plans are postponed because Harry has gambled away his money and is in dire straights. He tells me we must leave Toronto and go to Hamilton where he has a better-paying job. We leave immediately. Because we are penniless, we're allowed by the owner to move into a room at the rear of a Chinese laundry in Hamilton. I don't like this place; it's so bare, but I don't chastise my fiancé. I know he has taken a risk and lost. The only gambling I know of is the twenty-five-cent tickets with Chinese writing he buys. Sometimes he wins five dollars or more.

—

We're living behind a Chinese laundry in Hamilton. There's a Native Canadian woman living here with the laundryman. We exchange few words. My fiancé arrives from work very upset. My mother came to Hamilton and found him.

"She came into the restaurant," he says. "She acted terrible! She was yelling and hit me in front of the customers. She wanted to know where you were but I didn't tell her."

The next day we return to our previous quarters in Toronto, an old three-storey building in the rear of some stores. It's occupied by only an elderly Chinese man (who is out working most of the time).

Harry and I are having breakfast when there's a loud banging on the door. "Police! Open up!"

Two heavy policemen come in followed by my small white-faced father.

"Is that her?" the policeman beckons to my father.

"Yes, that's her," he answers.

The policeman turns to me. "Get dressed! You're coming with us!"

I look over at my fiancé. He's being his usual polite self, respectfully answering questions. He isn't being taken. It's only me they want.

CHAPTER 5

I sit in the back seat of the police car with the two policemen in front as we drive through the downtown traffic. We stop at the side of a huge building where I'm escorted into the basement and put into a barred cell.

In a short time a woman comes and the door is unlocked. She directs me up the stairs and along a hallway, off which are numerous doors. We stop at one with an extended sign that reads *Barrister*. I think, *Thank God, a lawyer has come to help me*. The room is empty. The woman sits behind a desk and questions me.

"How old are you?" she asks.

"Eighteen."

"What religion are you?" she enquires.

"Protestant."

"No, I mean what church do you belong to?"

I pause to explain. "I don't know. I was baptized Greek Orthodox. My mother belongs to the Church of England and I went to Sunday school there."

It's becoming clear that this lady isn't a lawyer. "Have you ever slept with anyone else besides the man you were living with?"

I hesitate. To save my boyfriend from blame I will have to damage my character.

"Two," I say.

"What are their names?"

I give them to her. I suspect I'm pregnant, and I volunteer the information, hoping it will force a marriage. When she hears this she closes her book and returns me to the lockup.

—

A policeman unlocks the door of my cage and we again climb the stairs. We walk a considerable distance and stop at a heavy ornate door. We enter a large room with benches on the left side. I look for my father but don't see anyone, only a middle-aged man facing me from a distance. His seat is raised and he appears to be sitting on a podium. The walls are bare. I'm in a courtroom and the man facing me is Judge Browne. I'm standing with my back to the door.

I become aware of a policeman halfway down on the left-hand side. He's stating the address where he found me, saying my fiancé's name and that he was wearing a bathrobe and that I was wearing pyjamas. I'm consumed with shame.

The judge asks, "Are you pregnant?"

"Yes."

"How far gone?"

"Three months. If you'll just let me out of here long enough, I'll get married."

My words have no effect. Without hesitation, Judge Browne says, "Remanded one week for sentence."

"Remanded for sentence"—what does that mean?

The policeman who had escorted me to the courtroom must have been standing behind me. Immediately after the judge's remarks, he takes my arm and brings me back. I hear him say to another policeman, "She loves him. Why won't they let her marry him?"

I walk back and forth in this barred cell in shock. How could it be that a judge, knowing I'm pregnant, would refuse to allow me to marry the father of my child?

—

*N*ow I'm taken down the same concrete steps and put through the back door of a large van I hear them call the "Black Maria." I'm locked in, the sole passenger. Inside this dim enclosure is a long board seat at either side.

My head and throat ache. I'm alone, trapped, and voiceless. I throw myself on the floor and scream hysterically. I toss about and start screaming, "Let me out!" I thrash about and bang on the sides of the van.

"Let me out!" I cry, over and over again.

A policeman peers in at me through the small wire-meshed window on the door.

"It won't do you any good—you can't get out," he says.

Nothing I can do will help. I feel the car moving out into the traffic and gaining momentum.

We stop at the jailhouse and climb the high steps to the reception office where I'm turned over to a guard and placed in one of a line of barred cells. I feel too distraught to take notice of anyone else who might be here.

I hold a dim hope that my fiancé might rescue me though I know it's impossible. A Chinese man can hardly come looking for a white woman without endangering himself.

I declared my immorality during the interview to protect my boyfriend. Otherwise he might have been charged with a morals offence.[1] But nothing, it seems, would have saved me.

—

The wooden bench on which I sit serves as my bed for a week and there's no change of clothes. No pillow or blanket is supplied. A male guard unlocks the door when I request access to the washroom. When walking through the corridor, my heel slips and I fall backward; I hope it will cause a miscarriage.

The jail doctor gives me an internal examination in a cramped examining room.

It appears that I'm the only woman. At mealtimes I'm directed down some narrow steps to the basement where I sit at a long splintered wooden table with men and eat greasy stew.

Silence pervades except for the occasional guard who walks through, looking in. There's nothing to read. I sit and think. Only my father or mother can free me from this place. When will my father come? Where's my mother? I don't understand. She's in control of all situations. Doesn't she even want to talk to me? Does she know I'm pregnant? Would she be able to tolerate her daughter being pregnant outside of marriage? I have heard her say of a friend who had an illegitimate child, "Esperance is weak-minded." According to my mother, any woman who can't deal with an unwanted pregnancy is a country bumpkin.

—

My father doesn't love me. He lost interest in me when he remarried. After the divorce, my mother left Saint John for Montreal to learn hairdressing. I was ten years old when my father placed me in Mount Carmel Convent, even though we are not Roman Catholic. "It's a respectable boarding school," he said.

I hated the place—I was unaccustomed to restrictions. My father was always at work and my mother played cards every night and slept till noon. Our maid was always young and undemanding. I told my father I didn't want to stay in the convent but he put his finger to his lips, demanding silence.

We were allowed out for a half-day each month. My brother picked me up and helped me onto the bar of his bicycle for the ride down the hill from the convent. My mother would write to me. When she told me how my father was marrying a woman who couldn't speak English, I cried and the nuns sympathized because they don't believe in divorce. I cried not because of the divorce but because my father's new wife doesn't speak English. I was hoping he would marry one of the waitresses who sometimes served me. An attractive blonde waitress had taken to waiting on me.

"How would you like it if I married your father?" she asked.

"That would be fine."

"Do you notice how your father follows me around?"

My father didn't tell me about his forthcoming marriage and I wasn't invited to the wedding. I was told to address his new wife as "Mrs." like a complete stranger.

My father was caught in a bind of divided loyalties. I was an interloper, someone to whom he had obligations. He pretended I belonged. At celebrations I was supposed to put in an appearance, enjoy myself, eat good food. But I felt lost in a sea of voices, a foreign language I didn't understand. I felt inadequate, diminished until someone for a moment benevolently addressed me in English.

My brother rebelled. He raged against my father's culture as backward and belittled his friends. "Greece is only a little country without a proper army," he sneered.

*

My mother must have contacted my father, knowing full well his weakness. "He's a coward," she would say. He is a coward. In one great frenzy of fear for his social position, he came all the way to Toronto and had me arrested. He wasn't even in court for my sentencing. He has dispatched me and gone comfortably home. How can my father, so kind and affectionate when I was small, turn against me so viciously?

Had my English grandmother seen the picture of my fiancé hidden under the mattress when I visited Saint John? Had she snitched to my father? I remember she had once rented a room to a couple and then looked in their luggage when they went out. She found they weren't married and evicted them. She remained in the room and turned her back while they packed. There would be no immorality under her roof. She's such a snoop!

The separation from my fiancé consumes me. I imagine I see him at every turn. How must he feel? I told him I might be pregnant. Harry must surely know I'm in impossible circumstances. He probably thinks I went back to Saint John with my father, under duress, of course, but even if he went to the police station, who would provide him with information?

I keep going over my situation, looking for clues to account for my arrest. Why did my mother not have me arrested? Why my father? She couldn't have known it was possible. What law have I broken? Did my mother just choose to frighten my father? She knows the disgrace he fears within his own community, for he would be appalled to have his daughter running off with an Oriental.

My mother can't be terribly afraid of this. She has no particular social standing to protect. So why doesn't she come to see me, use her wiles to free me? She can hardly remain angry over the altercation with my boyfriend—such volatile scenes are customary to her. She has won the battle, I've been found. Why is she not visiting me and using her influence on me to return home? Of course, she played a role in my apprehension but she couldn't have expected it to go so far. I've breached her authority but that's no longer important. She must know I'm pregnant—she would want me to have an abortion. She was never afraid I'd get pregnant perhaps because, before she was divorced, she had several self-induced abortions herself. She couldn't have known about the severe prejudice against the Chinese. Perhaps she can't get me out.

My mother has the feel of the downtown Church Street milieu. She doesn't for a moment believe I'm in danger of being influenced by sinister forces. She saw my boyfriend and knows he's working. My mother was never concerned with nationality.

However my father found out about my boyfriend, I can imagine that the police fuelled his feelings. Once a girl gets into Chinatown she's finished, according to them. They would fill my father with warnings about white slavery, vice, and drugs. All manner of evils would be laid at the feet of Chinese men.

These things could have been overcome. My father could have talked to me to ascertain if I was in danger. But he's not really concerned with my security. He's afraid that my association with a Chinese man will bring disgrace to his family. Only his own community is pure.

No doubt he learned the results of my court appearance. He hadn't apprehended me in time. I was pregnant. A Chinese grandchild! My God! I'd have to be put out of sight, at once.

My fiancé and I are in similar situations. Maybe that's what attracts us to each other. He's an outcast by virtue of his race. But I am also the object of discrimination. Because of my mother's divorce I am, like her, excluded from the world of stable, conforming families. The Chinese have been singled out by government legislation as undesirable and their families in China can't join them in Canada. Most of the Chinese here are men without mates and friendship with Canadian women is discouraged.

By statute the Chinese are singled out as the only people in Canada who cannot employ white women. My fiancé and I are lonely people who have found each other. We share the same enemies.

—

$\mathcal{D}$ays pass. I know my father won't tarry long in Toronto, but where's my mother? The possibility that my mother isn't going to rescue me occurs to me for the first time. I've been caught in a power struggle between two angry people—my parents. My father worked diligently to acquire a respectful place in the community. He's come a long way from the early days when my mother, a country girl, worked in his fledgling ice cream parlour. Her knowledge of the English language was an asset. There weren't many Greeks in the Maritimes then. When the business expanded and my mother's energies were no longer needed, she embarked on a vivid social life and became popular. My father wasn't interested and soon my mother became an obstacle to him. He started having affairs, which my mother learned about through the wife of his business partner.

My mother caught my father in our house with one of his waitresses. She had a witness, a male roomer. She had to "keep him company" to ensure his testimony in her divorce action against my father and his employee. Already, she was selling her favours—it was the price for leaving one's husband. She must have been terrified. Failure would have meant returning to my father's house and his insults and humiliation. To leave would mean she'd risk losing her children; my father could also have used my mother's "unwomanly" behaviour to have her committed to a mental institution.

There's a refuge called the Interprovincial Home for Young Women at Coverdale, near Moncton in New Brunswick. It's a Protestant home for women and girls from New Brunswick, Nova Scotia, and Prince Edward Island. A good number of those sentenced are older married women and girls who had committed an offence. But in Ontario, the *Female Refuges Act* allows an innocent woman to be confined, not for a crime but for being "incorrigible" or "idle and dissolute."[2] Could a man put his wife in a refuge?

The loss of respect, the humiliation, still torments my mother. I know the extent of her despair and I cringe for my future. When the time was ripe she set the trap. He arrived and did her bidding. My incarceration at his hands is her victory. It's he who put his daughter in prison. Now she's holding the whip. As long as I'm here, she can plague him with my unhappiness, blackmail him to ensure secrecy, and guilt him mercilessly. "He'll pay for his sins, he'll come crawling to me some day, and I'll have no mercy," she always vowed. My father can no longer laugh at her. No one must know he has a daughter in prison or that she's pregnant by a Chinese.

I imagine going back to his community, screaming to the rooftops about what he's done to me, but then I would be mad just like my mother. He did the best he could, he'd say. I'm no longer his daughter. But he can't escape the blood ties of a Chinese grandchild.

It's unlikely my mother could have foreseen the escalation of my plight, the ruthlessness of the law. How does she feel about my pregnancy? Is revenge against my father worth keeping me in jail?

CHAPTER 6

*M*y week at the jail is up and I'm again put into the Black Maria for my return trip to the courthouse. The date is May 10, 1939, which will be seared in my mind forever. I'm brought into court and stand in the same place. The judge says, "You are charged with being 'incorrigible' and I sentence you to one year in the Belmont Home."

I walk back and forth in this barred enclosure, stunned! How could it be that a judge, knowing I was pregnant, would refuse to allow me to marry the father of my child?

Yet it's so obvious—why hadn't I thought of it before? I know that Chinese are not allowed to bring their families to Canada. Chinese babies are undesirable. What could be worse than a white woman willing to challenge government policy designed to "protect" her?

I know that nationality is determined by the heritage of one's father. I hated it in school when I had to identify myself as Greek on the school register when my mother was respectably English and all my friends were British.

—

I'm put into the back seat of a police car and taken to a large house that resembles a rectory in a residential neighbourhood. After official documents are signed and the police have left, Miss Pollock, the superintendent, takes me upstairs and shows me my sleeping quarters. I'm in a room with six beds at the back of the building.

Then she takes me to the basement and shows me the toilet cubicles and tells me which ones to use, and not to use the one for a girl with venereal disease.

After that, I'm deposited in a large room with several occupants. Although I'm suspicious of my surroundings, being released from behind bars comes as a surprise. I sit edgily on a hard chair and feel my arm. It still hurts from the firm grasp of the policeman.

A young woman approaches and speaks to me. I ignore her. My being here is a mistake, an injustice. I'm fully aware of racial discrimination. The others are here for breaking the law. I can't believe anyone else would be here who hasn't been stealing or doing violent things. Bad girls are shrill and coarse, but I've never even spoken back to my parents.

My eyes are drawn to the only activity in the room. A tall gangly girl is standing behind the chair of another girl, arranging her auburn hair which is curled under in a page boy. I will learn that the red-haired girl is a minister's daughter from another Ontario city.

I've been sitting quietly with my thoughts for some time when a large number of girls pour into the room, talking freely. At the sound of a bell they crowd together at the top of the basement stairs. I'm now agreeable to getting up from the chair to fit into the routine. The girl who approached me has not taken offence, and I join her. She tells me that the girls have just come back from the laundry where they work. We're going downstairs for supper. I can hear someone saying, "We're having peanut butter." There's a certain exhilaration at this prospect.

We file down the narrow stairs to a large dining area. In it are several long tables covered with white tablecloths. I follow my friend to the table at the rear wall and stand while a supervisor says grace. On the table are white and brown buttered slices of bread and large bowls of peanut butter.

No sooner have we sat down than there's a commotion. I hear a strangled sound. It's at the furthest table and the girls raise themselves, trying to see what is happening.

"Victoria is having a fit," someone says, and I can see a matron moving hurriedly toward the front table. Another girl explains, "She's having an epileptic fit, they're putting a spoon in her mouth so she won't swallow her tongue." I can't move. I grit my teeth, suppressing a desire to scream.

As suddenly as it has begun, the crisis is over, and the meal soberly resumes.

—

*P*erhaps because I'm thin and pregnant I'm put on light housework duty. I have undergone an internal examination by a male doctor at the jail and, now at the Home, other aspects of my body are being considered by a woman doctor. Having completed another internal examination she takes a blood test, then she takes my blood pressure, examines my eyes, and inspects my teeth for cavities. I have barely eaten since my arrest. The doctor remarks, "You weigh only ninety-three pounds—you're undernourished. I'm going to prescribe calcium for you."

Sue, a twenty-four-year-old girl in a later stage of pregnancy, and I work together mopping the hardwood floors, dusting, and cleaning generally. I also work in a laundry room folding sheets with another girl as they come ironed out of a large mangle. Sue tells me she has two children and is expecting a third. She's very pretty with brown hair and eyes and a turned up nose; she's somewhat plump with a cheerful disposition.

Possibly due to her maturity, I become attracted to her. She tells me that she married a man who turned out to be a bigamist with whom she had her first child. Then she lived with a different man and had the second child. When she became pregnant with her third child he abandoned her. I imagine the rest. It's common knowledge that a woman living with a man out of wedlock can be reported to the Children's Aid. She is providing an "immoral" environment for her children. She could be charged with contributing to delinquency.

Sue smiles as she describes the antics of her children. She laughs with embarrassment as she admits, "I like a little nookie sometimes."

My views of the type of person placed in a home begin to change drastically. There are lots of different women here, but we all have been imprisoned under the broad label of immorality. Whether this covers vagrancy or prostitution, who's to say? For the most part, it seems we have just been plucked out of our homes.

The Belmont is definitely not a home for unmarried mothers. I figure there are possibly sixty inmates; only four of us are pregnant. There are no babies about. All the girls I meet have been sentenced to two years for being incorrigible. My sentence of one year is unusual.

My mother visits me. It's the first time since my arrest. She smiles and describes her latest accomplishment. "I spoke to the judge. He was going to give you two years but I persuaded him to give you only one."

I can believe that. My mother's experience as a fortune-teller includes palliating her clientele as well as giving advice. She's an expert at manipulation. It doesn't take much imagination to figure out that my mother has convinced the judge I'll give up my Chinese baby and return home.

I don't ask what transpired between her and my father. It's a subject to be avoided to spare her guilt. We both know she played a role and that she acts on the spur of the moment.

I wonder if, in her anger, my mother exaggerated my unorthodox behaviour and maligned my character? Most self-righteous citizens would condemn me. God knows, the criminal tag of "exclusion" in the *Chinese Immigration Act* is a euphemism for "undesirable." I'm debased by association with an undesirable.

I know my father is directly responsible for my being here. He laid the charges, not my mother. But she has convinced herself she's in charge of the situation. She suggests that my brother doesn't want me in the house. She intimates that he doesn't feel I'm fit to be at home in my condition. She must cater to his wishes. She's caught between us but will cater to his wishes. Of course, if I were free I would not be in her house. I'd be with my boyfriend, but this isn't discussed by either of us.

I will never extricate details from her concerning my arrest. When she doesn't want to answer she lets her mind wander. I learned never to repeat a question. "Never cry over spilt milk," she always says.

—

*I*t's not clear even to me why I detoured so far from popular views. During my childhood I absorbed all the myths and values of my community. How did I get here?

I remember being in Saint John, walking to school along the cracked cement sidewalk of Union Street. No step or grassy surface intervenes between the narrow street and stores or houses. Overhead wires that supply electricity and extend between pockmarked wooden poles are covered with sparrows. At an intersection I can see the gravestones of the settlers who remained loyal to Britain during the American Revolution. As I walk past the drab wooden-slatted houses, I peer into the windows, which are always dark and unrewarding. I discover a door and enter a long narrow passageway between old houses. It opens onto a large untamed scrub-grass area that appears to be the backyard of several decaying and fallen buildings. I pull open the creaky door of what looks like a chicken coop and find an outhouse with two holes in the wooden seat. So old and unused is the outhouse that even the flies have left.

There's no sign of life, not even an empty bottle can be seen. This is not a haven for the destitute of our seafaring town. Union Street is somewhat removed from the harbour where the cheap flop houses, clandestine activity, and loud discord occur. Maybe this neighbourhood has been left behind by even the worst-off rural migrants who came to a city that couldn't even support its existing population.

Spying a large black ribbon on a door, I cautiously open the door, leaving it ajar in case I have to run. In a beautiful polished wooden coffin lies an old woman with white hair, eyes closed, hands clasped. Dressed in white, she looks very grand and peaceful. I smile—I'm not afraid of the dead.

Neither am I afraid of snakes; my mother took me to a fair and the snake man put one around my neck.

I remember too, Miss McGee's grade one classroom with its thirty wooden desks on the first floor of the square red-brick elementary school. The class is all girls. The rough boys all have their own play areas. Rules have to be followed. Even on freezing days we have to wait till the bell rings when we line up to enter school. We must all put on our coats, overshoes, and scarves and go out during recess regardless of the weather. Our seats in class reflect our school marks. The girls in the first row appear to be dressed better that the others and tend to play with one another. The girl in the last seat in the last row always looks frumpy and I don't play with her. I'm annoyed that June Robinson is in the first row. She's black and I'm convinced she cannot be smarter than me. I'm in the first seat in the third row.

For misbehaviour, Miss McGee wields a hard wooden ruler right onto an open hand. One of the most awful things that happened was when Myrtle Askey wet herself while standing in line.

Miss McAllister, our grade two teacher, is different. She'll take a girl into the cloakroom, set her on her knee, and talk quietly. The girl will come out flush-faced and teary-eyed. Sometimes it seems that Miss McAllister is giving the girls turns in the classroom to induce confessions rather than for misbehaviour. During our confidential talks I tell her my mother smokes. She gives me a note to take home. It says that by smoking, my mother is setting a bad example for her daughter. My mother becomes angry. She says, "I'm going to report Miss McAllister to the school board." To emphasize the teacher's prudishness, she declares, "Miss McAllister is an old maid!" even though we all know that married women aren't permitted to be teachers.

On the way home from school, a small Chinese man with a bulky white bag slung over his back comes towards me. He's been collecting dirty linen for laundering but it's rumoured that he will grab little girls and stuff them into his bag. I cross the street long before he approaches. In the window of a fortune-telling store I pass is a large coloured drawing of a human skull with small wriggly compartments and a big yellow picture of the palm of a hand with red, uneven lines. The inside of the store is concealed by heavy gold and red drapes. Sometimes gypsy girls with dangling earrings and bright costumes move the drapes and peer out. It's a place to beware of because everyone knows the gypsies will steal everything you've got. I skirt an alley while watching apprehensively lest some dark miscrants appear—it's the only place blacks can obtain accommodation. The lane is locally called "Nigger Alley."

Perhaps loneliness and freedom from supervision draw me to always be friends with the poor kids.

—

*L*inda, my mother's friend, reveals nothing of her present life to my mother but then neither do I. My mother trusts me; she feels I'm capable of taking care of myself. She sees my independence as no different from hers, but both Linda and I know that our lives are different from my mother's since we're crossing a racial line that society condemns.

Linda takes me to her Chinese boyfriend's place in the back of a decrepit-looking house. Through the door we enter directly into Jack's quarters. It consists of two rooms, one being a small kitchen with a sink. I figure the bathroom is upstairs. He's probably living in a Chinese rooming house where it's cheaper to share the rent, lock the doors, and avoid unsafe contacts. Jack's English is not as good as Harry's and other waiters', nor does his brown pants and blue shirt suggest a waiter's occupation. It's likely that Jack works in the kitchen of a Chinese restaurant. If he worked in a laundry he would have a room in the back or upstairs. No longer is a laundry designated a factory so that cooking and sleeping on the premises are forbidden. At one time, workers who broke the rules would be fined.

I'm probably the first guest that Linda has brought to Jack's place. Linda smiles and says with a flourish, "Jack, this is my friend, Velma."

Jack says hello with a broad smile. It's easy to see the affection between them. When Linda puts her arm around Jack, the whole world shimmers. She brings in the outside world of excitement and novelty. Her presence makes his lonely bachelor life worthwhile. Jack is radiant and Linda is proud of her lover.

But they never go out together, and Linda has another home where she spends time. Jack doesn't question Linda. He trusts her and knows she cares. She's dependable—she'll always come back. The affair has been going on for ten years. Linda's family is upper class and they live in another city. Jack is Linda's anchor in her escape from the conventional life she knew.

Is that why I'm here, then? Because I'm unconventional? In Belmont, I learn that girls like me are "incorrigible," though since we had homes we're not classed as vagrants. Is this a blessing? All the Belmont girls have stories. They are spread from one girl to another. We assess our own degradation by comparing ourselves to each other. The length of a sentence doesn't really reflect our misdemeanours or society's revenge. Here, no one devalues me because of my Chinese boyfriend, just as no one criticizes the girl involved in incest. Social condemnation doesn't extend to our captive enclave.

I become friendly with the girl who has epilepsy. She's fourteen years old, small, and fragile with fair hair and blue eyes. Her favourite song is "Beautiful, beautiful blue eyes." Often I hear her singing it. She says, "My parents put me here because they're afraid I'll run off and get married like my sister."

One unhappy-looking round-faced girl remains aloof and speaks sparingly. Someone tells me she's Hungarian, also fourteen years old, and in for incest with her brothers. Even if she was born in Canada, like any person of foreign parentage, she will be described by her parents' nationality.

Probably because she is also pregnant and because she's so honestly outgoing, I begin to form a close relationship with Helga. She's tall, fair, and broad-shouldered, and although fifteen years old, can easily pass for twenty. She says, "I was put here for going around with a married man." The way she says it indicates the ruling belief that marriage is a lifelong state. I hear her repeat the statement to others—it's made without expression. She exhibits no guilt. There's a certain obstinacy about Helga; she'd be prepared to challenge the law and run off with her lover. Her serious countenance, clean-cut features, and athletic build project firmness. She has a slight hearing defect that may account for her thoughtful manner. She's in an early stage of pregnancy, her condition likely hidden from neighbours by her family.

As the days go by I come to know more girls. By her conversation, I can only presume that one particular girl has been arrested and charged with being an inmate of a bawdy house. She insists she had been drugged and kidnapped. "Nobody will believe me because I'm not good-looking," she tells me. It's true. She's not especially attractive but she's tall and has a good figure.

I'm the last girl to arrive at the Home until a disturbed willowy girl is admitted. She has just given birth. Because she is underage her parents have signed her baby away. She's obsessed with the baby she's lost and talks about it continuously.

As she wanders off, sympathy for her ordeal invites an exchange of grievances by those of us who are sitting nearby. One of the girls has located herself in one of two upholstered chairs. Another girl and I are each sitting on one of the numerous hard-backed chairs around the periphery of the room. It's now evening and we're relaxing after our day's work. The girls have formed their friendships and are gathered together in small groups.

Myrtle, who is sitting closest to me, says: "I was transferred here from the Ontario Hospital School at Cobourg. I was put there by a social worker—she came to our house and took me when my mother was taken to the mental hospital at 999 Queen Street. The next day she brought me to the Children's Clinic at the Toronto Family Court where I was examined by a psychiatrist. I think the doctor believed I inherited mental problems from my mother. I was ten years old."[1]

"It's a terrible disgrace to have a relative at 999. Why were you transferred here?" I ask.

"I don't know. The Hospital School is supposed to be for people with borderline intelligence. The name's going to be changed to Cobourg Training School."

"Borderline—what's that?" a girl asks.

"A little bit retarded, I guess. I'm sixteen," the girl continues. "Old enough to be apprenticed as a maid but I want to go and stay with my mother when she gets out of 999. Sometimes she gets better. I've been back with her a couple of times."

"What happens if you're with an employer you don't like?" I ask.

"I don't know but if you complained maybe they'd put you somewhere else. But if you run away and they catch you, you're put in the Mercer Reformatory; they say it's a terrible place."

The other girl intercepts. "An industrial school doesn't have to take girls back if they run away, especially if they're older. The school takes in girls as young as seven and they think the older girls are disruptive."

"Maybe that's why they send them to the Belmont," I say.

I wonder at Myrtle's naiveté, mentioning her deranged mother. I feel a certain distance from this girl but I don't like these feelings. What if someone felt superior to me? Her transfer to the Belmont Home may be seen as an advancement and her previous time at Cobourg an embarrassing mistake. She must feel good about that.

My mother told me that Mrs. Underhill, who rented a room in our house, had been in the Whitby Asylum so I never spoke to her. I was afraid of her. When she moved out she left behind a trunk full of pretty china dishes.

"I was thirteen when they took me," said another girl. "My father left us and my mother started living with another man—you can't sleep with a man you're not married to. My mother was considered to be setting a bad example for her daughter. The Children's Aid worker asked me if they occupied the same bedroom and I admitted it. But now I wish I'd said no. Then to make matters worse, someone told the judge I'd been seen on the streets at night when my mother was working. My mother and I were in the Juvenile Court and the judge said to my mother, 'You are exposing your daughter to lead an idle and dissolute life, and contributing to juvenile delinquency.' I was charged with being incorrigible and sent to the Galt Home for Girls. My mother came to see me but she couldn't get me out. I was there for over two years. I was so mad. I wouldn't do anything, just fooled around in school. The superintendent said I was unmanageable and they sent me here. So now I have to work in the laundry."

My heart stirs for these girls. Why have they been so rudely removed from their relatives and friends, and for such minor offences?

The drawing room in which we're located is divided into two sections with an archway between. One could have imagined that it was designed as a parlour with an adjoining dining room in a large mansion. Some of the girls are sitting at a dining-room table at the back, playing cards. Others have gone upstairs to their rooms. There's a sofa and a good number of hard-backed chairs. The large window at the front is the only one that's not covered with hard-wire grating. It has blue drapes on the side and a curtain of a flimsy material at the centre through which one can see the front gate. The door to the office at the front from which we'd been admitted is always locked. It seems that the church women at the Belmont have tried to make the place as homey as possible in the circumstances and are reasonably sincere in their efforts at rehabilitation.

"I'm not here because I was transferred from a Home," I say. "I was sentenced in adult court. I'm eighteen, old enough to get married."

"Wouldn't your boyfriend marry you?" a girl asks.

"Sure, but we didn't know I could be arrested, so we didn't get married in time."

"How old do you have to be to be sent here?" She asks.

"I think you're supposed to be fifteen," someone says.

"Mildred's not fifteen yet," a girl interjects, "but some of the girls here are really old."

Just then the superintendent comes into the parlour. "Miss Pollock, why are some of the girls here so old?"

"Oh, that's because they've been here so long, they don't want to leave."

—

*C*hurch services are held in the chapel on Sundays by Salvation Army women in uniforms. They always play on the piano, "O Lamb of God I Come." Occasionally during the singing, a girl gets up from her seat and walks down the aisle to be saved. We are made to understand that this is the equivalent of giving one's life to Christ. A girl who steps forward is met by two Salvation Army women who put their arms around her.

One day a Salvation Army woman says, "You girls don't know how lucky you are. In the Mercer Reformatory the girls must remain silent. All that can be heard is the clanging of doors." What, I ask myself, is the Mercer Reformatory? And why is she mentioning it to us?

I ask a girl, "What's the Mercer Reformatory?"

"It's a prison for women," she says. "They say it's a terrible place—it's called a house of horrors. Just thinking about it gives me the willies."

—

*W*e arise one morning to find several girls missing—they didn't even appear at breakfast. Speculation runs high as the names of our missing friends are bandied about. Have they been released? Where have they gone?

The next morning more girls are missing. Panic spreads among us. It's apparent we're being moved, but where? Furthermore, although it's midweek, girls are not being sent to work in the laundry.

During the afternoon, I'm ushered along with several other girls into the superintendent's office. Miss Pollock tells us. "The Home is closing down and all the girls are being transferred to the Mercer Reformatory."

At the mention of the Mercer, some of the girls start crying. "You're going to be all right," says Miss Pollock. "You will be well cared for there."

That's it. Our tolerable confinement in the Home is now terminated. We must now prepare ourselves for servitude in a place we've heard horror stories about. We descend the wooden steps of the Belmont Home and climb into the back seats of two private cars.

CHAPTER 7

I've been in custody for over three months, several weeks in the Mercer. It has been bearable, but now something frightening is happening. A severe case of vaginitis has suddenly come on me. I can't sleep from the itching and burning. Cold water from the tap fails to alleviate the terrible discomfort. I ask Miss Miles for time off from the factory to see the doctor. She sends me upstairs to the nurse.

Nurse McGrath is in the hall near the door of the examining room. I explain my distress. She says, "The doctor is away, and only she can help you." The nurse's words are absolute. I cannot argue. I must wait for the doctor. I've reported my condition and she has given me the standard response.

It's evening and I'm locked into my cell. I feel as if my whole body is turning rotten, but I can't call out for attention. It would be improper. I'm trapped in this little space and there's no relief.

Several days pass. I'm getting worse. Something strange is happening. I can see several narrow growths extending from my labia. I again accost the nurse. With great embarrassment I tell Miss McGrath that there's something growing down there.

On that day, we're just starting work and the machines are buzzing when we are bade to be silent. Miss Miles is reading from a list, "The following girls are to report to the doctor." My name is among those called.

Thank God, the day has arrived. I'll finally get medical relief. There's a good dint in the number of factory workers; the sewing machines lie idle as we leave our stations and head upstairs to the doctor's treatment room on the third floor.

Already there are about twenty girls in the hallway wearing the white leggings and tops. The doctor's assistant, Miss Allison, opens the door to the clinic and calls out a name. A girl goes in, the previous one having left. I figure a girl comes out every three minutes or so. No one is allowed to have a watch, and there's no clock. Time is governed by the orders of our superiors. Although the doctor proceeds quickly, there's waiting time for most of us.

My time comes and I get onto the table. I know I'm in trouble because of the symptoms, but it would be impertinent to disrupt the doctor for information. My condition has become visibly abhorrent and I expect the doctor will be shocked.

But there's no apparent reaction. She merely says, "I see you have warts."

I watch as she opens and closes a metal box at her right. I don't think anything about it until I feel excruciating pain. My hands clench the table. I lie there obediently, barely moving. The operation is interrupted while there's another opening and closing of the metal box and a quick mopping up. I'm convinced it's over.

Suddenly I feel a pain so encompassing that I lose all control. My hands tear loose and flail about. The doctor says to Miss Allison, "Hold her hands." She complies by crossing my hands at the wrists and bearing down with all her weight.

Then, with one swift motion, the doctor applies a burning liquid. My body lurches forward as if stung. The pain is so intense that it takes me a moment to realize I'm being told to get down just after this.

I can hardly sit up. The assistant has my arm and is helping me off the table. I can't stand up but am bent over. The doctor says, "I don't want you to eat any tomatoes." The assistant opens the door to facilitate my leaving. As I go out the doctor firmly repeats, "Be sure you don't eat any tomatoes!"

I hobble into the hall oblivious to any girls who might still be waiting. I try to gather my clothes off the floor where I'd left them. They keep falling from my hands. Finally, I manage to hold them long enough to put them on. The pain is intense. I'm thinking this can't be true. Things like this don't happen in Canada. A person can't be tortured to death without someone saying a word.

A matron appears and says, "Come with me." Across the hall and east of the treatment room, she unlocks a door. It's left slightly open to provide light to a narrow wooden stairway. The matron directs me down the stairs while she follows behind. At the bottom of the stairway she takes out another key and unlocks a heavy wooden door. We enter a dim low corridor.

The tomb into which I'm to be sequestered is the first one in the corridor almost opposite the stairs. The matron again opens a solid-looking door. This chamber is larger than the cell I've known but I'm in too much pain to care. The matron stands aside as I enter, then she locks me in and leaves.

I see a dusty, single iron bedstead with a coiled bedspring and mount myself on it in a kneeling position and rock back and forth. The wire cuts into my knees and for one brief moment I lie on my back.

Extending along the ceiling and slightly below are two vertical lead pipes about two feet long leading into a horizontal one. At either end are openings for gas emission. They're going to kill me!

No, why would they treat me if they're going to do that? The gas jets must be for fumigation. I know gas is used to kill bedbugs and germs. It doesn't occur to me that the pipes may have been left over from the time before electricity was introduced, when gas lighting was used.

I get off the bed and kneel on the dusty floor. I continue to rock back and forth to ease the burning for what seems like hours. Finally, a matron unlocks the door, hands me some bedding, and leaves.

The burning goes on but is beginning to ease up. I think it must be suppertime. I've had no dinner today, the kitchen staff wouldn't have known I was here. I couldn't have eaten anyway.

I'm in a high-ceilinged room with an iron-barred rectangular window. I'm in the front of the building, probably on the second floor, facing the street at a distance. The place is bare except for a bed, a table, and chair. There's a bathroom with a large tub. Except for the bathroom, the place is thick with dust. It would seem that no one has been here for years. Why, I wonder, if I'm supposed to be sick, am I being put into this dirty place?

My speculations are interrupted by someone calling me through a slot in the door. I can't see who it is, but only a matron would have a key to the corridor.

I receive my supper passed through the slot at the bottom of the door: two half slices of bread, a pat of butter, and cornstarch pudding on a tin plate with a spoon. There's no conversation. She's gone. There's no tea—a cup would not likely go through the slot. It must be inconvenient for a busy matron to bring food up to the third floor and then down the narrow steps to my quarters.

In the morning the area that the doctor treated is protruding, black, and swollen. The burned appearance of the skin must have been caused by an acid. Until the swelling goes down in a few days, walking is awkward.

I find a *Good Housekeeping* magazine. How did it get here? I've never seen a magazine in the Mercer. The pictures reveal a luxury I can only dream about in my grim surroundings. I'm in solitary, shunned. There will be no book distribution here. I'm not acquainted with the idea of quarantine. No matron will step into my unwelcome quarters, but then neither does a matron enter a cell. I can now turn the light off and on at will. I spend my time looking out of the window and rereading the magazine.

It's morning and someone is calling me through the slot. I go to receive my breakfast. It's bread on a tin pie plate, nothing more. A hot cereal can hardly be offered, which means I don't get the skim milk at the bottom of the bowl. The noon meal is excellent and bread is included but I can't get a second helping.

I've counted the days to seven and know this is treatment day. Aside from the pain and the burning, I'm unaware of what the doctor was doing to me. I have to believe she was excising the warts but I don't know what caused the overwhelming pain. The acid must have been used to cauterize the wounds. I come to this conclusion much later after a movie I saw. In the film a man on a ship in the old days had his leg removed below the knee and a hot iron was applied to the stump. The man screamed. Why the doctor would use such a primitive method of treatment, I don't know, but it would save time and not likely require a dressing. It would be a long time before I will see the medical record. In it, Dr. Guest reports using Argyrol, a "soothing antiseptic."

A matron bids me to come forward and follows me upstairs. She hands me my hospital attire and tells me to be quick. There are only a few girls left waiting in the hall, the others obviously having gone back to work. I don't think anyone knows I've come up from isolation—no one saw me emerge with the matron through the obscure door. It's down the hall from where they're assembled. They wouldn't even know a door existed in such a place. It's said that detention cells for unruly inmates are located in the basement. I don't want anyone to know I'm in isolation. No one needs to be curious or fearful of my unhealthy plight.

All the girls have been in and out of the clinic and gone downstairs. I'm alone in the hall and the last girl is dressing when Miss Allison calls my name. I climb onto the table and put my feet in the stirrups. The doctor, as before, is sitting at the bottom of the table. I'm convinced that the offensive tissues have been removed, that surgery occurs only once, so I await evaluation. But I'm unprepared for what ensues!

I see the doctor open a metal container on the left-hand side and a gush of steam pours forth. I know instantly that the container is used to sterilize instruments. Then by holding prongs with her right hand, the doctor retrieves a pair of surgical scissors. I'm terrified, what's she going to do with them? I gasp as I suddenly realize that what happened before is going to happen again. I panic—she's going to perform surgery on me, not a simple one where a boil is lanced by one swift insertion of a knife, but one that requires multiple excisions by scissors.

A great pain assails me. I grope for the sides of the table and hang on tightly to withstand the assault. As the surgery continues I hear my voice becoming audible. I'm unable to remain silent. Then there's the wait—I have twisted myself at such an angle I can see the doctor. She has bent her head and is adjusting a hypodermic needle, barely below my line of vision. Is that why I couldn't see before? Perhaps the doctor doesn't want me to tell anyone. Why would she be giving me an injection in soft tissues? The nurse in anticipation has already crossed my wrists and the doctor looks up at her knowingly. Still holding me tightly, Miss Allison extends her body backward to watch the doctor. I flounder and cry out. Then the doctor, with one wave of her hand, brandishes a chemical brew over the exposed bleeding flesh. I hobble out of the room, dress, and am returned to isolation.

When I'm able to move about the room again, in a corner covered with dust I find a small book. The paper cover, formerly white or beige, is discoloured and the pages are yellow with age. It's a Catholic story and tells of a girl who said one thousand Hail Marys and got her wish. I remember the rosary from when I was a child in the convent. Although I disliked the convent, I adjusted to the routine and grew to believe in the Roman Catholic faith. I now follow the example of the girl in the story. God must hear me—my plea is deserving. I pray that the warts will go away.

Hail Mary full of grace,
The Lord is with thee,
Blessed art thou among women,
And blessed is the fruit of thy womb, Jesus.
Holy Mary, Mother of God,
Pray for us sinners now,
And at the hour of our death, Amen.

It's hard to keep count. Without a rosary to aid me I make strokes in the dust on the windowsill. The barred windows are never opened.

A week passes and again my door is unlocked. I ascend the high steps to the hallway fearfully. Although I've said a thousand Hail Marys I'm not trusting.

I'm having difficulty keeping still and cry out when cut. I'm aware of the dreadful moment of acute pain when my body loses all endurance. The injections are the worst. This treatment has been as bad as the others. The Hail Marys didn't help. I'll never believe in God again.

⸺

*R*eceiving food is the only interruption to the silent isolation of this place. Today, supper is bread with a pat of butter. The voice outside says, "You're not allowed to have tomatoes." I'm vaguely aware that farming is carried on somewhere on the grounds. There must be a good crop of tomatoes, because bread—without tomatoes—is becoming a standard supper. The *Good Housekeeping* magazine is filled with pictures of food and I imagine tasting it. My appetite is voracious, probably due to my pregnancy but then I don't allow myself to think of that.

I can see the street from the window. It's a long way off and people seldom pass. The figures look black and I can't tell if they're men or women. I hope someone will look this way, though it's unlikely someone can see me behind the bars. What would anyone think if they knew of my agony? They walk by, perhaps thinking of a love affair or some other matter which seems so trivial in comparison. Love, now so distant, appears to me as a luxurious fantasy compared to my life of physical fear. Each passerby looks straight ahead; no one ever turns to look at the Mercer.

The matron has unlocked the door for my customary descent into Hades. As I emerge from my involuntary seclusion, I catch a glimpse of Helga, her head bent, unseeing, being entombed at the other end of the musty corridor. She's being placed into quarters on the same side of the corridor as I am. This is the first time I see her but she could have been here all along. The other side of this corridor is bare wall. Some sparse hint of daylight must be entering this deserted passage but I can't see from where. Only fifteen, what a pity! It's unlikely she knows I'm her neighbour. Who would tell her?

As I ascend into the wide hallway near the medical room, I find the place deserted. The girls must have been treated and left so there will be no witnesses to hear my cries. Helga must have been the last patient before me. We are the two Belmont girls least advanced in our pregnancies. Sue will have had her baby by now and be in the nursery. Elsie, the tall redhead, will be having her baby any day now.

I know it's still summer by the trees and foliage I see from the window. Still, some leaves are turning yellow. My birthday is in early September and I don't know if I've turned nineteen yet.

I haven't gotten into the bathtub although there's hot water. No one told me I could take a bath, and I could be scolded if the doctor disapproved. Anyhow, I don't want to touch myself. I can't face knowing in advance what might happen, can't face losing faith that each treatment is my last. I'm sustained by hope in order to walk through the door of the medical room.

When I feel the pinch of squeezed skin being severed, I groan louder. It's easy to see why someone in battle would rather die than be caught. To be shot would be so easy. I'm angry with the doctor—why doesn't she give me an anesthetic? Because she won't take the time. I've never been put to sleep before but I know such pain should be avoided. I'm unaware that each written request for anaesthetic must be submitted to prison authorities. I learn later that any removed tissues have to be turned over to the pathology department. How is it possible that I haven't had a miscarriage?

A matron unlocks the door, hands me clean clothing, and tells me to take a bath and put the clean clothes on. "Don't touch anything," she says. I'm coming out of isolation—I must be cured. How long have I been here? I've counted four treatments, at least a month.

It's noon and I go to the dining room. No one asks me where I've been, and neither do I feel disposed to tell. As we only whisper to the girl next to us, I don't know the girls across the table.

I occupy the same cell as before. I'm relieved to find that little Victoria, so pale and thin with constant epileptic seizures, has gone from the ward. Perhaps she's been sent to the Woodstock Hospital for Epileptics or to the Orillia Hospital for the Feeble-minded. The Belmont Home had compassionately accepted Victoria.

I go back to work on the power machine. The girls have graduated to making flannelette pyjamas. The air is loaded with lint that gets in my nose. The antiquated machines are over twenty years old, having been installed in 1915. My machine keeps breaking down but I'm loathe to complain. There's something wrong with the bobbin and the threads keep bunching up. I keep undoing them. My mind is gripped with awful memory and apprehension and I can barely function. Miss Miles is gaining the attention of the class. She's holding up the pyjamas I made and says, "It's taken this girl a whole week to make one pair of pyjamas." There's a slight titter from the girls. I don't feel responsive to the intended humiliation.

I'm heavily pregnant as I get up from my machine to obtain some material. "You should be ashamed of yourself," Miss Miles says. "Go and sit down at once." I grasp the reason for her embarrassment. A man is nearby repairing the machines.

―

J encounter Helga near the doctor's room the following week. She has also come out of isolation. We're the last two patients, which bodes ill. The doctor will be spending more time with us.

We find we're suffering from the same affliction. Helga's name is called and I remain alone in the hallway. It seems she is gone for twenty minutes or more. I see her come out with flushed face and tired eyes. "It hurts so much," she says. I'm immediately called in. When I return, Helga is gone. Later, when I see Helga in the recreation yard, she tells me she had gone downstairs after treatment and out into the yard where the girls had assembled after dinner. "The burning was so bad, all the girls came round and asked me what was wrong." I'm amazed by Helga who is youthful and so gregarious.

My inability to confide my pain to others has added to my isolation. I envy those who are so brave, those with the courage to speak openly—not to worry what others think. I prefer to hide away.

Miss Milne has just returned from holiday. Now she will see Miss Miles's record of my absence from work. Nurse McGrath's records will also indicate I was not in the infirmary. Miss Milne will learn that I was in quarantine for a whole month. What must the superintendent think?

―

*M*y release from isolation has not changed my treatment. I dress and shuffle to my cell. A matron seeing me there locks the cell door. A matron knows when she sees a girl in a cell that she must be locked up, no questions asked. I'll miss my dinner and supper but it doesn't matter. The burning persists for hours so my mind is not on food. A matron seldom passes through the corridor. I'm not likely to see one again. No one comes to inquire if I'm well enough to go downstairs for supper. Besides, it would be extraordinary for a girl to be wandering into the dining room alone. The matron has no time for individual concern.

Supper is over and the girls are arriving. They're free to talk in the corridor for half an hour or more. The time seems to vary depending on how busy the matron is, I suppose, or perhaps some matrons are more lenient than others. Anyway, we don't really know because there's no way of measuring time. There's no recognition of a particular matron for any supervised task. Having escorted the girls to their ward, the matron immediately disappears. She probably didn't see me in my cell. I didn't try to get her attention to let me out for a spell and she wouldn't know if I should be freed. She'll come back later delivering her order that the girls enter their cells for lockup.

My mother visits me. She says she came to see me earlier but was turned away. She doesn't go into detail and I say nothing about my time in isolation.

I'm so desperate I throw myself on her mercy. It's a change in our relationship. I've never talked to her before about my feelings or about life outside our home. This proves difficult, however, because my mother is not interested in conversations in which she doesn't play the leading role. I have to be blunt, almost yell at her, "The doctor is cutting me with scissors! I can't stand it, you have to get me out!"

I'm accustomed to her digressions—she acts as though she doesn't hear me. My suffering probably adds to her expectation that I'll have a miscarriage or the baby won't be born alive.

She attempts to steer our conversation into a more pleasant direction. "I sold the rooming house and I bought a house on St. David Street. We play poker every Saturday night. I caught Mrs. Shroeder taking money out of the pot when she's supposed to be putting it in," she says brightly. "Alex, a shoemaker, he's Italian, always comes over. He's sweet on Linda."

I refuse to be detoured and continue to plead for help. My mother gets up to leave. For all her valour, her confidence may be wavering. Matters where I'm concerned must be seen in a new light. I may be beyond retrieval. Or she may be unable to obliterate my dire experience and return me to the fold. Neither is she prepared to challenge the prison and medical bureaucracies.

Further, she knows that my release would mean a return to my fiancé. She would lose all her influence over me. For me to be released on the eve of giving birth would create problems. She will likely relate my shameful medical condition to my brother and father for solution. There will be no compassion. On the contrary: it will reinforce their belief that I properly belong in prison.

If anyone is going to help me, it's my mother. But despite her willingness to enter the Mercer to visit me, she's showing no signs of behaving any better than my father.

We're allowed to write a letter to a relative twice a month. I write to my father asking him to come and see me. If he knows my plight he might have pity. I'm careful in what I say because I know it's censored. There's no reply.

—

There's been enough public propaganda to guess why we're on the doctor's list. Do all these girls have gonorrhea? It's a subject that's never discussed. I dare to ask one girl. "What are you being treated for?"

"Whites," she says.

How does she know that? I wouldn't think the doctor would spend time treating a girl merely for a white discharge. Only the girls with syphilis would know for sure what they have. The girls in Galt Training School take douches. Why isn't it done here? I never hear a girl say she has taken a douche. It would require absences from work and extra vigilance by a matron. When I'm approached to take my weekly bath in the big bathtub on the first floor, I'm told to hurry back.

Whatever the doctor is doing is beyond question. Being called up to fall in line is a presumption of venereal disease. For us Belmont girls it's the ultimate disgrace. We younger girls don't talk about it. The less said the better.

I develop abdominal pains of anxiety. This has been happening regularly almost from the beginning. I don't want to be offensive on the table.

This day as I'm entering the medical room, the doctor is sitting at a small desk on the right across from the bottom of the examining table. She looks up from her notes and declares, "This is the worst case of gonorrhea warts I've ever come across!"

Looking back at her notes she exclaims in astonishment, "This girl has been infected twice!" The doctor raises her head, observing

Miss Allison closing the door. It was unlikely she heard the last remark.

So I do have gonorrhea, just as I thought. I must have a malignant type, so when the warts are gone I'll be cured.

But what does she mean, "infected twice?" How could I have been infected twice? How could the doctor fathom that? And I had no symptoms of disease before being arrested, neither in the jail nor during my six weeks or more in the Belmont Home. How can this be?

Prior to my surgery I'm now being treated internally, a quick painless procedure. I'm in my last month of pregnancy and extremely uncooperative.

"Try saying a little prayer," the doctor suggests.

"God has forsaken me."

"Well, keep still. I don't care about you, I care about the baby that's going to be born!" the doctor says angrily.

As the medical assistant helps me off the table, there's a knock at the door. It's noon so perhaps the doctor has a luncheon engagement.

As usual, I'm bent over and in great pain. The doctor beckons Miss Allison to hide me in the washroom around the corner on the right.

Miss Allison proceeds to close the door, leaving me in the dark. Then she changes her mind and turns on the light. There's a toilet and a basin in the small washroom. Staff have proper washrooms. Mercer toilets have neither seats nor doors. When I emerge the doctor says, "It will have to be disinfected."

I shuffle into the empty hall, dress, and go to my cell.

I'm rocking back and forth from the burning when the matron who locked me up unexpectedly returns. She unlocks the padlock, opens the door, and offers me a china cup and saucer and says kindly, "I thought you might like a cup of tea." I take the tea from her and thank her with a forced smile. It's the first fine cup and saucer I've seen since my arrest. The tea is sweet with cream—a luxurious treat. I know the matron has sneaked it to me from staff quarters. Food isn't allowed in the cells, let alone tea.

Although I'm in too much pain to enjoy it, I drink the illicit nectar. The matron soon comes back and whisks away the forbidden dishes. It means nothing to me that I forego nourishment on treatment days. It's too insignificant to even consider. But this is the first display of kindness I've known by a matron.

CHAPTER 8

*T*here's an older woman, probably in her thirties, sitting next to me in the dining room. She's the first older woman who has sat at our table. She tells me she's in for thirty days. "If I have venereal disease I'll have to stay longer," she says. She's the first person I've met who has broached the subject. Why don't they know if she has VD? She's the only one I've met with a thirty-day sentence. I wonder if she's telling the truth.

The next day I meet another girl; she's very pretty and says she's Jewish. She says she's in for picking up men in cars and is an epileptic. How dangerous! But how can an epileptic ever hold a job?

The dining room is silent and all the girls are looking towards Miss Milne who is secluded from the inmates by her raised chair. She's saying, "Get back and sit down!" I stand up to see the object of her anger, a tall young woman with an earnest face. The girl is saying, "I just want to talk to you" as she advances slowly towards the superintendent. We other girls sit frightened and spellbound as we witness this daring behaviour. There are no matrons about to protect the superintendent, and of course we're glued to our seats in amazement. Miss Milne continues to repeat firmly, "Get back and sit down!" The girl hesitates and pleads, "But I only want to talk to you." Then the girl gives up. Tension breaks as she returns to her seat. It's rare to see such open defiance. I decide that she must be a drug addict.

—

*M*y mother visits me again. She tells me she's opened a second-hand clothing store on Queen Street. "I read teacups now by appointment only. I put an ad in the paper with the heading, 'Why worry?'"

She no longer tries to be entertaining as she knows I'm not listening. She must be aware I'll be going into hospital soon to give birth but this isn't discussed. The word *baby* is never mentioned. I don't think about it either. I don't anticipate the future. I exist only for myself in the present. I have no feelings but fear. The disgrace of being pregnant out of wedlock and the physical pain I've experienced blot out any consideration for my baby.

—

*T*his is the first time I've been to the Mercer beauty parlour. We're supposed to get our hair washed once a month but because I was in solitary I missed it. As I enter I pass a large mirror. It's the first time I've seen myself since being apprehended. No one is allowed to have a mirror. My eyes are staring back at me, unbelieving. The mirror reveals my distorted figure and my eyes look defeated. I have the same hunted look of the silent incest girl from the Belmont Home.

A girl wearing a white smock takes me to a sink and washes my hair. We don't talk and I don't know if she's a Mercer girl. She could be a girl in training sent in to practise from hairdressing school.

After leaving the beauty parlour I see someone I know, a gracious Polish lady, in an unfamiliar corridor. I first met her in the yard and I felt then that she was looked on as someone apart, deserving particular respect. "What are you doing here?" I ask.

"I'm coming from English class," she answers.

I'm not sure I heard right for I've never heard of a class in here. Perhaps the classes are for those who are illiterate. But usually inmates are not permitted to have paper or pencil. She's a special case—I read about her in the newspapers before I was arrested. She shot her husband for seducing her niece, but he didn't die. She was sentenced to two years. She may be in her thirties. I realize I've never seen her in the treatment line. In fact, I've never seen an older woman there.

Years later, I find out what Mr. Nixon, the provincial secretary, said to justify the Belmont girls being sent to the Mercer: "Girls who are illiterate are given elementary academic schooling...girls are taken in groups or individually if they are particularly retarded." This hardly applies to the Belmont girls. Those I meet appear to be Canadian-born and have been through school like I have.

I say, "Are you going back with your husband when you get out?" She answers politely, "I don't know," and moves on.

I see a Catholic chapel through a nearby door. I wonder if this Polish lady is coming from there. I imagine she has a good rapport with the priest who will be able to intercede on her behalf. I think of the Salvation

Army women at the services. What influence would they have in their line of hierarchy to help Mercer inmates? I don't believe they can help me.

For church service on Sunday we each wear a mauve dress with short sleeves and white collar and cuffs. It's worn only once and then laundered. As at the Belmont Home, services at the Mercer are conducted by Salvation Army women. Each Sunday we say the prayer of confession to expiate our sinful behaviour. I find it hard not to say the melodious droning words:

> Almighty and most merciful Father,
> We have erred and strayed from thy ways like lost sheep,
> We have followed too much the devices and desires of our own
>   hearts,
> We have offended against thy holy laws
> We have left undone those things which we ought to have done
> And we have done those things which we ought not to have done,
> And there is no health in us.
> But thou, O Lord, have mercy upon us, miserable offenders.
> Spare thou them, which confess their faults.
> Restore thou them that are penitent;
> According to thy promises declared unto mankind
>   in Christ Jesus, Our Lord.
> And grant O most merciful Father, for his sake,
> That we may hereafter live a godly, righteous, and sober life,
> To the glory of thy holy Name. Amen.

Every Sunday I repeat these words. But I'm not penitent. I will never be convinced my sentence is just.

—

The sound of my accursed name being called out in the factory brings instant dejection. Only when my name is no longer called will my treatment be ended.

I trudge wearily up the stairs. Girls from various workstations mount the stairs in disarray. For a pregnant woman, ascending the stairs in a monitored lineup is exhausting. The ceiling is towering and the curved stairway has many high steps. We round the second landing and plod laboriously to the third floor. I look over the banister. It's a long way to the bottom—throwing oneself down must be the hardest thing a pregnant woman could do.

Some girls already assembled are complaining that the instrument has burned them. It wasn't sufficiently cooled off before insertion. An athletic-looking girl with short fair hair is sitting on the floor near the door to the medical room, crying. We ask what's wrong. She doesn't answer but keeps on crying. Another girl explains, "She's scared because she's a virgin."

When she goes in we wait uneasily. Shortly, she comes bounding out and grabs her clothes. "What happened?"

"The doctor told me to get down off the table," is all she says as she dashes away.

I've never heard a girl criticize another except once when an older girl came to me and pointed to another who was walking along the corridor. She said, "She has syphilis so bad her hair's falling out, stay away from her." I look at the girl, a tall handsome young woman with full lips. I guess she's of Slav origin. She's staring straight ahead. Later I hear she attempted suicide. I cannot bring such rejection on myself by discussing my treatment. I sit on the floor waiting.

I share my father's faith in the prophets of science. He always ridiculed my mother's spiritual preoccupations and I silently agreed. Now I find myself thinking heretical thoughts. The doctor is certainly cruel but is she lacking in integrity? How can this continual surgery be necessary? Does my body sprout fleshy tissue that must be excised weekly? What if I touched myself—would the spell be broken? What if the doctor knew I was suspicious? How much worse would it be if I challenged her? Why do I cooperate? Why don't I stand up for myself and say, "If you are saving my life—don't! Just let me die!"

⟶

Today is different. Only my name and that of another girl are called out in the factory to attend the clinic. We are the only ones ascending the two flights of stairs, past the second floor where wards remain vacant during the day, and onto the third floor.

The wide hallway where the girls usually assemble is deserted. The door to the clinic is open so the doctor must be waiting. Dr. Guest peers through the open door and invites the other girl to come in. The girl emerges shortly, dresses, and is ready to go downstairs before I am called in.

The doctor says, "Get on the table." Miss Allison is nowhere about and it's awfully silent without her. Dr. Guest is handling her patients alone today. She's not, as usual, stationed at the bottom of the table but rather stands beside me, thinking. Is there something wrong? Has my treatment not progressed satisfactorily?

It feels strange to be alone with the doctor. I lie still. Her nearness and our seclusion in this confined space create a sense of familiarity in contrast to the impersonality I've come to know. What's more, she isn't wearing her white coat. Rigid formality seems to be replaced by casualness. She's so close I could reach out and touch her. My throat is dry and I feel uncomfortable. Suddenly the doctor's expression resumes its usual tenor. She quickly packs the vagina with saturated cotton and says, "Just lie there and don't get up." She quickly leaves the room. I'm sure she's in a hurry. Is this the reason for my reprieve?

I'm relieved I won't have to go through the terrible surgery and injection. But now I'm experiencing a terrible burning, this time in the vagina. I'm sure the material has been soaked in the same cauterizing agent used on me before.

I feel the time elapse slowly as the burning intensifies. I'm burning up! When will the doctor return?

The time stretches interminably. How long have I been here—one hour, two? I'm facing the window. Will the sky turn dark before she comes back?

The burning is intense. I may have escaped the scissors and needle but am I any better off? Has the doctor forgotten me? No, that's not possible, she never makes mistakes.

My mind wanders. I'm thinking, enduring, accepting. My mind is focused only on the immediate future.

I hear someone come in and turn my head. Nurse McGrath is looking for something in the cupboard near the door. She turns around and is clearly shocked when she sees me. "What are you doing there?" she asks.

"The doctor told me to lie here and not get up."

Miss McGrath is mystified. She tiptoes uncertainly to the bottom of the table, takes some prongs, and removes the offending material. I go to recover in my cell.

I'm in my cell for some time before a matron passes by and locks me up. I'm still confined to my cell when the girls arrive after supper. There's free time to talk, then the matron arrives with the customary demand that the girls enter their cells. One by one each girl is locked in for the night and the ward is silent.

CHAPTER 9

A dull pain in my lower back is occurring at regular intervals. I'm in labour—what will they think at the hospital when they see that I'm all black inside? I bang my door back and forth; soon the other girls join in. A matron comes quickly and with little explanation unlocks my cell and escorts me downstairs.

A car takes me to Burnside, the maternity wing of the Toronto General Hospital, where I'm wheeled into a small room and placed on a table. A nurse comes into the room occasionally to assess my condition and leaves; otherwise I remain alone. The hospital is quiet. I know it is night.

In the morning, a tall man dressed in white and wearing a white mask comes into my room through an adjoining door. This is my opportunity. I address him, "Doctor, I have gonorrhea—take care of the baby's eyes." I don't realize that for decades it's been hospital policy to put silver nitrate into babies' eyes. Blindness from gonorrhea has been almost eliminated.

The doctor remains, looking at me skeptically through penetrating dark eyes. Then without a word he walks back into the room from which he emerged.

In the afternoon I'm transferred to the delivery room and put to sleep. I am roused once, but soon sink back into sleep.

When I awaken I'm in a semi-private room. The other bed is unoccupied. After awhile a nurse brings my baby to me for nursing. The baby is a boy. He looks dark and tawny and I find the situation strange. I have never held a baby in my arms.

This is my first time in hospital and, not knowing the protocol, I hardly venture from my room. I assume it's not allowed.

A young doctor comes in. He says pleasantly, "Now you have a son to raise and put through university."

"He'll never see university," I answer.

"You never know," he says. "Here's today's newspaper, perhaps you'd like something to read."

"Thank you."

It's a delight to read a newspaper again. It's the *Globe and Mail*, dated October 17, 1939. After reading the war news I turn to the women's section. The heading says, "Names of Two Hundred Women among Immortals." Imagine! There's Dr. Guest's name! She was presiding over a tea put on by the University Women's Club at Exhibition Park yesterday. So I was right—she *was* in a hurry. And she didn't get back in time to prevent Miss McGrath from finding me.

My mother doesn't come to see me in hospital and I know why. I'm in hospital having a baby whom she does not want to see. What would she say if anyone questioned her? What would she tell my brother or her boyfriend? She would never stand for personal ridicule. I've always been tainted in the eyes of my father's family because of my mother's shortcomings. Now she will be forever humiliated by racism directed against her daughter and grandchild.

———

I've been alone here for twelve days. The nurse says I'll be leaving tomorrow. That means I must return to the Mercer. My weekly medical trials never end and I'm afraid of what awaits me. I feel a sympathy and fondness for my baby but my fear is overwhelming. I must escape.

It's evening and my baby has been nursed. I'm dressed in the short hospital gown and slippers. I tie a sheet around myself, go to the elevator, and descend to the basement.

The basement is large and eerie. I can hear voices in some distant part. I look for a door, find the delivery entrance, and walk up the entrance to the street. I run towards Bay Street, a commercial area.

It's late evening and there are few people on the street. A man driving an old car stops. "What do you think this is, Hallowe'en?"

My mind is sharp in desperation, "Someone made me a bet I wouldn't go out dressed like this."

I get into his car. "Where can we go?" he asks.

"We can go to my place."

I direct him to my fiancé's address some blocks away. The radio is on. I'm so afraid, I'm convinced I hear the words, "escape" and "hospital" on the radio, so I talk quickly to distract this unsavoury-looking person.

He stops the car and I ask him to wait as I go in. The entrance to my former quarters is through a yard at the back of a building. My boyfriend may be there.

The place is in complete darkness; nevertheless I climb the wooden steps and knock on the door.

It's futile. I'll have to go to my mother's. I return to the parked car and get in.

"I can't get in the building; I know another place."

The unkempt man says, "What's going on, what are you trying to pull off? Go on, get out of here!"

He drives off and I look for a store. I beg the clerk, "I have no money, please let me use your phone, it's an emergency."

My mother has moved since I've been in prison, so I look in the phone book and find her number. When I reach her, I hysterically demand that she help me. My mother is her old self, responding calmly to an emergency. I'm to take a taxi and she'll be waiting for me.

Although it's night she finds a doctor to see me. The doctor is alone at his office which is located in his home. My mother explains that I have been maltreated—will he examine me? When he hears the story of where I've been, he refuses.

My mother says, "You must go back—I'll write to the doctor and tell her not to hurt you anymore." I'm crying and pleading with her but I have no alternative.

At the hospital I'm placed in a wheelchair, taken to a basement room with wire netting on the windows, and put to bed. A young nurse sits with me.

I talk incessantly. "I used to be like you," I tell the nurse. I describe my medical treatment, the scissors and injections that haunt me. The nurse leaves and returns with a glass of water and two tiny white pills. I take them and remember nothing more.

In the morning I'm taken to a waiting car and handed my baby wrapped in a blanket for the return trip to the Mercer.

I carry my baby upstairs to the nursery on the third floor. The nursery consists of a large room off which a hallway extends to the rooms for mothers and infants. Another hallway off the nursery leads to the wider hallway and hospital area. A door opens onto the closed-in veranda where the babies remain during the day. The rooms are big enough to accommodate a single bed and bassinette. There's no water in the rooms but hot and cold water can be obtained from a sink nearby. In contrast to my cell, there's a door and a window. The baby and I are locked into our sparse quarters.

Being locked up all day is punishment for my escaping and deters me from talking to the other inmates. The time hangs heavy. Soon I will have to see the doctor. Again, I feel I must I escape.

I save my three-pronged fork from a meal brought in and ease it into the upper part of my stomach. It's difficult until I puncture the skin. Now the going is easier but I'm afraid to go too far. I don't want to die—I have my fiancé and my baby to live for—I just want to return to the hospital where it's safe.

I manage to insert the fork a good half-inch. A matron, coming round to lock the mothers in the rooms for the night, looks in on me. I imagine I have done enough damage and show her the wound. She immediately contacts the superintendent who comes hurrying to my room.

Miss Milne asks, "What have you done?" so I show her.

She leaves and returns almost immediately with a bottle of iodine. "Lie down," she says as she soaks the injury with the antiseptic.

She's angry. "We try to make it so the girls can go to the hospital to have their babies. It's girls like you who spoil it for the others. You know you could get five years in the penitentiary for deserting a child."

"I would have come back when I was cured," I say plaintively.

Miss Milne, continuing to saturate the wound, sits beside me and listens. I tell her of my trials and my terror. Suddenly, there's a change in her attitude. "You won't have to see the doctor right away," she tells me.

I refute her words. "Yes, I will," I say dejectedly. I don't believe her. I don't believe she has that much authority. The doctor doesn't have to consult the superintendent on medical matters. Why should she?

Miss Milne is spending so much time tending me, I feel a certain dissonance. Why do I warrant all this attention?

As she is leaving she becomes solicitous, "Would you like something to read?"

"No thanks," I murmur.

As she walks out the door, Miss Milne says defiantly, "I promise you, you won't see the doctor for a month."

The determination in the superintendent's voice should have alerted me. Miss Milne believed she had some authority to supersede Dr. Guest's medical power. What could it be? Miss Milne had been Dr. Guest's nurse before she was promoted to superintendent, possibly with the doctor's recommendation. Disagreement could be traitorous. To what extent did Miss Milne dare rebel? What weapon could the superintendent use to express dissent? (Dr. Guest had been one of a number of visiting physicians to the Belmont Home. There was a Mrs. J. Milne on the executive of the Belmont.)

The following day my food is served on a tin plate instead of a dish, with a spoon replacing a fork. I find this amusing. It's probably standard practice for girls who attempt suicide.

I'm being released into my new routine, working and caring for my baby. I nurse and change him, wrap him in a blanket, and place him on the cool veranda to sleep, then leave for work. During the morning I return from work, retrieve him from the porch, nurse, bathe, and dress him and then replace him on the porch until the next nursing session.

I notice my son gets a rash from the warm bath water; the rash later disappears. I don't mention it. There are prejudicial beliefs about Orientals and I don't want to bring any negative attention to my baby.

The mothers arrive at the nursery at the same time during the morning to nurse their babies. There's no matron about and we are able to talk freely.

"How long were you in hospital?" asks Sue.

"Twelve days," I say.

"Did you have stitches?"

"I don't know," I answer. "I was sleeping."

"Sleeping?" Sue says, exchanging glances with Elsie.

"The chart at the bottom of my bed said 'episiotomy'" I say.

"That's it," says Sue, "you had stitches."

I say nothing but the thought occurs to me that the chemical treatment I endured before birth may have impeded my baby's entry into the world. Why was this done? Was it to sterilize the birth canal?

—

*S*ue had her baby, a boy, about two months ago. She says she'll be going to court—something to do with the baby.

Nursing mothers are provided with a jar of milk and a piece of buttered bread in the evening before retiring. The bread is passed out first. I get my bread and put it on the hot radiator in my room. The cockroaches that dot the wall extend their fangs toward the enticing delicacy. I get my milk and enjoy the repast sitting in bed. The cockroaches can't get onto the crib or the bed because they can't climb up the metal legs. Ever since a cockroach got into my old Mercer slipper, I keep my slippers on my bed.

This morning Dr. Guest is passing through the nursery accompanied by Miss Allison. The mood here is cheerful and most people are solicitous towards the babies. The doctor enters my room saying, "What a nice ba..." then stops and remarks solemnly "but not quite an English baby."

It's my mother's first visit since returning me to the hospital. She says, "I wrote to the doctor and told her she's not to hurt you anymore." She looks worried. An escape from prison is serious—it might add more time to my sentence. Should I be charged, would she have to appear in court?

"The house was full of police when I got back home," she says.

During my tense escape my baby hadn't been mentioned. She doesn't ask any questions, whether I had a boy or a girl, but I don't doubt she phoned the hospital for particulars. I avoid the subject.

Finally she asks me, "Are you going to give the baby up?"

"No."

"Well then I'm not coming back to see you anymore," she replies and abruptly leaves.

—

My baby is about one month old when Miss Allison says, "The doctor wants to know if you want your baby circumcised."

"Yes," I say. "I do."

A few days later a matron comes towards me at noon and says tersely, "You're to go up to the nursery and tend to your baby."

I climb the two flights of stairs as quickly as I can. A matron is waiting for me. She removes the cotton diaper and reveals the reason for my summons. My baby's penis is distended and swollen.

I'm dismayed. How could such a calamity occur so suddenly? The matron tells me to apply warm compresses to allay the swelling. I feel so sorry for my baby and assiduously obey her instructions. I'm engrossed in alleviating his pain and don't go downstairs for supper.

For some reason, Miss Miles from the factory is locking us up for the night. "Miss Miles," I ask, "Could you leave my door open tonight so I can reach the hot water tap? I have to apply hot compresses to the baby." I forgot Miss Miles's embarrassment over the repairman when I was pregnant and want to impress her with the urgency of my request. I remove the cover for her to see. She opens her eyes wide, turns her back, and quickly walks away.

———

*T*he month is up. I put on my leggings and wait. "This is the girl we have to use a lot of painkiller on," says Dr. Guest cheerfully as I walk in.

I feel a liquid being poured on my private parts. The doctor sits waiting for it to take effect. I expect the worst and I resist. The doctor must assist Miss Allison to hold me down.

I have no faith in painkillers and scream as the cold metal scissors devour my flesh. When the operation ends, Dr. Guest says, "This is the last I'm going through this." How does she know that? How does she know what my future condition will be?

This time, I'm not subjected to the all-engulfing pain of the injection nor the burning chemical. The doctor may be sensitive to the medical complaints I made as reason for my escape.

I see Miss Allison in the nursery the following morning. She's not only the doctor's assistant but also supervising matron of the nursery. "Look, look!" she says to me indignantly, "You put your fingernails right through my wrist—look at the scratches." I don't look. I feel contempt that she thinks her minor pain is so important, and that she seems so unaware of mine. I expect she would agree with the doctor, that my pain is justified, but hers is undeserved.

———

I accept the doctor's word—that was the last time. This week there's merely a quick painting of the uterus. This treatment continues the following week. I relax, safe at last.

Helga has arrived in the nursery with a baby boy. She's such a methodical and devoted mother. I'm apprehensive for her. Nature has given her a body and maturity beyond her years but she's bound by government regulations. Her married lover is also bound by strict divorce laws. I don't know if she's sixteen, the age in Ontario deemed to be beyond childhood. Her age, together with her slight hearing defect, will make her vulnerable. The Child Welfare people will surely force her to surrender her baby unless her parents help. She never mentions them.

I know she will fight to keep her baby. I imagine she can be obstinate, perhaps from being demeaned for her handicap.

I see Sue in the nursery crying. She has been to court. "My boyfriend brought in two men to say they'd been with me. They're taking my two children and leaving me with the last one." Sue's cheery nature is gone. She moves like an automaton and doesn't talk anymore. There seems to be a shadow over her eyes.

A new mother has arrived in the nursery with her baby boy. She's much older than the rest of us but it doesn't matter, we're all the same here. We are now five mothers in the nursery: the four Belmont girls and the other girl who has come in. The new arrival is married and has several children. Her name is Pearl. She's mild and placid and doesn't mind telling us she abhors her husband's insistence on anal intercourse.

Miss Allison confronts us mothers with the new ruling. We will no longer be permitted to bathe our babies. This activity will be taken over by Pearl, the new mother in the nursery.

Elsie, the tall redhead with a baby girl and the most imperious, says, "I want to bathe my own baby. I don't want anyone else doing it."

Miss Allison, who had seemed to appreciate Elsie's independent manner, now exercises her authority. "It has been decided that the mothers will no longer bathe their babies," she says firmly.

Elsie is more sophisticated than the others and I've always felt intimidated by her. She has a know-it-all attitude. We're not friendly with each other but there's no animosity either. Elsie has a good-sized baby girl and she's very fond of her. In fact, the baby is her whole life. She continues to argue against the new edict. I fear conflict with authority— a challenge that can only bring dreadful punishment. How can Elsie dare to speak back?

The argument unnerves me and I start screaming. Miss Allison is alarmed. She says, "Stop! Stop that screaming at once!" She slaps my face hard but I can't stop. Miss Allison grabs a pillow and hands it to me, "Put your head into it!" she demands. I do what I'm told but keep sobbing until it eventually subsides.

When I go to work in the morning I can't find my bedspread. Miss Allison tells me to go along anyway. Later she says, "Do you know where I found your bedspread? It was under your mattress."

I feel embarrassed at the nurse's remarks, that I have done something highly irrational. Why now, when the worst is over, am I reacting in a nonsensical way? Is this a reaction of my exhausted body to the assaults that have gone before? Miss Allison is looking at me quizzically, curious. My deviation from normal behaviour has undoubtedly been reported. I am being watched, more so since my escape, apparent attempted suicide, and hysterical screaming. I am only a step away from madness. I must be careful, check every movement so there will be no repetition.

———

*W*e inmates are going to see a psychiatrist. This is a novelty and we make a joke of it. As I enter his office, Dr. Hills, a tall lank man probably in his forties, is slouched in a chair with legs extended and hands clasped between his thighs. I find this posture odd and wonder if it has any sexual connotation—does he think I am so predisposed?

He shows me a drawing of a circle. "If you lost a ball in that field, how would you go about finding it?" he asks.

I answer, "I would start at the outside and go round and round until I reached the middle.

"What are you going to do when you get out?"

I'm going to marry the father of my baby."

"Why are you throwing yourself away?

"Do you mean because he's Chinese?"

"Well, yes."

"That's racial discrimination," I say. "You're prejudiced."

"But didn't you see any boys in high school that you liked, someone better looking?"

"No."

I don't mention the high-school boy I drank cokes and smoked cigarettes with at a corner store because I wasn't attracted to him. The only thing that stands out was my surprise when the boy said, "Some of my friends say I shouldn't go round with you because you're not white but you're the whitest girl I ever met." He knew my father was Greek; this would never happen if I lived with my mother.

The psychiatrist continues. "You must realize you will be isolated if you marry him."

"I'll take that chance," I say.

A week later I see a woman psychiatrist, perhaps in her thirties. She asks, "what are you going to do when you get out?"

I answer, "I'm going to marry the father of my baby."

"Do you ever read the newspapers?" she enquires.

"Yes, before I came here I used to read them all the time. We're not allowed to have them in here."

"Yes, I know," she says. "How far did you go in school?"

"I passed with honours into high school."

"And with ease," she replies.

CHAPTER 10

A matron approaches me. "Come this way," she says, and I follow. We ascend the two flights of stairs, turn left, and walk along the hall. We stop at a door near the end of the hall, across from the stairs to the isolation cells. She knocks on the door. A voice from within says, "Come in." She presents me to the doctor who is sitting behind a large desk to the left of the window and leaves. The office is large and pleasant. I'm surprised. I didn't know the doctor had an office.

Dr. Guest invites me to sit down on the chair facing her. The chair has a soft seat and curved arms. I accept this generous offer.

The doctor says affably, "I want you to take some pills—they will make you better."

My heart skips a beat, terrified. I thought I was better, but now the warts might come back? Why is the doctor asking me? Why am I not just being told what to do?

"Will you take them?" she asks. "Yes," I say because to refuse would be unthinkable.

"Then you will take them," she repeats, smiling.

"Yes, I will." I'm thinking she has a beautiful smile. Besides how dare I say no?

As I come out of the dining room after meals, a matron is waiting for me with a glass of water in one hand and a fair-sized pill in the other.

I don't expect anything to happen to me from a pill. I'm nursing my baby but I'm not worried. It doesn't occur to me that the drug might pass into the breast milk.

Each time the matron gives me a pill, she watches me swallow. We adhere to this routine for several days by which time I'm extremely dizzy and nauseated.

I'm at the dinner table when I bolt for the toilet and am sick. Did Miss Milne see me get up from the table and run, breaking the rules? I can't take any more pills so I report to the doctor. She enquires about the effects I experienced. Her manner is brusque; she's displeased. Am I guilty for not keeping more pills down?

—

We're the last three girls waiting to see the doctor on treatment day. Either we have come too late or I don't see the last girl go into the examining room. Miss McGrath unexpectedly emerges. She quickly closes the door and, with an expression of solemn intent, runs up the hall. It's unusual to see a prim, mature person like Miss MGrath in such a dither. Where's Miss Allison? She must be with the doctor behind the closed door. I usually see Miss McGrath way up at the end of the hall where the medical supplies and the infirmary are located. She comes back and re-enters the medical room but immediately comes out again and races up the corridor. I can't see what she's carrying back. Miss McGrath barely closed the door behind her when she reopens it and addresses us, "The doctor will not be seeing anyone else today."

Rumours abound among the inmates who speculate about what happened. One girl who manages to keep track of the days says it happened on December 11.

The following Monday, Dr. Guest is gone and Dr. Hills, the psychiatrist, has replaced her. I'm surprised to see him there. Still apprehensive of this hospital setting, I lie on the table nervously. At his touch I jump involuntarily and begin to cry. This is the last visit to the doctor's office. I'm discharged.

—

My mother's decision not to visit me again is forgotten. She's beaming and gets up from the chair in the visiting room as I enter. I know exactly what she thinks—leave it alone and the whole matter will work itself out. I can hear my mother reading teacups, "I see you overcoming difficulties." With her optimism she's a sought-after teacup reader.

Today, she has a special tidbit to relate. Nothing can keep her away, she must get my reaction. She has reached the pinnacle of her queendom. "Roy and Bob had a fight over me," she says merrily.

The fistfight happened in the entrance hallway. Roy is my mother's steady boyfriend, whom I like, and Bob is the challenger. I know him slightly. She tells me she chose Bob and abandoned Roy. "But why didn't you choose Roy?" I ask.

"I couldn't do that," she exclaims. "Bob was the winner, I have to choose the winner," she laughs.

———

*J*t's said that the matrons will be serving us in the dining room on Christmas day. This is indeed true. They rush around bringing us plates of roast pork with gravy, potatoes, and vegetables. We can eat all we want and get additional helpings from the serving counter at the distant left of my table. I give myself another helping of everything—I've been starved. At each place is a large net bag with candy and an orange and apple. I've forgotten what fruit tastes like. The rule of silence has been lifted and the long lonely hours we spend in our cells are forgotten.

There's a loud buzz of excitement as the girls openly talk and laugh and get up from their seats to curiously join those huddled in animated conversation. Even the usually stern expression on Miss Milne's face as she sits on her high chair appears softened. The emotional release also brings with it turmoil, memory of family ties, and guilt. The spirit of Christmas invites expectations. One of the girls has broken down and is crying over separation from her children.

"Look at me," another girl tells her. "You're not the only one."

———

*"Y*ou're not to go up to the nursery tonight, you're to go to your cell," a matron orders and walks away.

I run after her. "Why, why?"

"Your baby has been taken to the hospital," she says and resumes her pace.

I'm alarmed—why has he been taken to the hospital? He seemed all right this morning when I left. Who to ask? I don't dream I have access to Miss Milne.

I'm unable to go to the nursery to search out anyone who might know anything, not that anyone would be there who could help. We live in a "don't know" world and a matron must never divulge information or even speak to an inmate unnecessarily. Furthermore, I don't have permission to go to the nursery. I would be breaking the rules and dare not imagine what punishment would be levied. I can't wander about the Mercer on my own volition. The memory of physical pain has robbed me of all strength and initiative. So who can I ask about my baby?

I can't ask my mother to find out what's wrong. She doesn't want to know anything about the baby.

The day is over and I make my way to my former cell. We're locked in for the night and I'm crying. A voice calls from another cell. "Shut up!"

I feel my heart shrivel. What place is this that my tears can bring such a vile response? I don't know what cell the angry voice came from. It must be someone hard-hearted and without compassion. It's hard to believe that even in here a girl could have no sympathy for another. The cruel response has jolted me. Why am I crying? Tears are wasted in this place. A girl cries here only when physically provoked, or like Sue when she just got back from court, or myself, suffering from shock.

Continuous sorrow, an impossible state, gets replaced by numbness and resentment. Am I to become bereft of feeling like some others? Will I now become angry and revengeful?

The following day I'm directed to go to the dispensary for Epsom salts to dry up the milk in my breasts. I must take it for three days consecutively. At the dispensary a matron is standing behind a counter, doling out medication. About six girls are lined up ahead of me. I receive the nasty Epsom salt crystals and drink them down with some water. I notice the girls ahead of me receiving pills of various sizes and wonder why they're taking them. Later I ask someone who says, "They're getting laxatives."

The return to my cell feels permanent. I don't anticipate my baby's return from hospital. I begin to feel a vague resistance to the idea of his return to the Mercer. In comparison to the Mercer, the hospital is a safe place.

I don't speculate on what's wrong with my baby. I was no longer bathing him and don't think about the rash. I remember only that he seemed well enough. The injections I received from Dr. Guest must have been necessary. I have no knowledge of serious illness except for my brother's infantile paralysis.

I don't see any connection between my health problems and the baby's health. My mother told me that Cherie's boyfriend kicked her in the stomach when she was pregnant. (Cherie was the French-Canadian woman who roomed in our house.) I'm under the impression that nothing but a strong blow can damage an unborn child. My mother said that my brother was born with two thumbs because she had a scare when she was pregnant, but she's inconsistent. She also said that the

King of Greece was born with two thumbs, suggesting that my brother may have inherited royal blood.

Still I grieve for the loss of my baby. I compensate myself with the observation that the babies here are pale and expressionless—they never get outside the closed veranda. The babies who remain bound and waiting for their mothers to retrieve them may not always be sleeping.

I reflect disparagingly on myself and the other mothers. Who among us is capable of eliciting a spontaneous smile from our little ones? Not serious Helga who has experienced the same trauma as I have, not Sue who has lost her children, let alone me—I am still maimed from terror. Even Pearl is dull and expressionless. Only Elsie, I think, retains a measure of confidence and attempts to get a response from her daughter.

———

A dentist is visiting the Mercer. Inmates can attend, though it is not compulsory. I am waiting in the inevitable lineup outside the dental clinic where inmates hurriedly emerge, handkerchiefs clutched to their faces, fumbling toward their vacated work stations. They have tarried too long. I'm having a wisdom tooth extracted. The pain will be different from what I'm accustomed to: not the sensation of a steel implement squeezing and cutting, or the continuous buzzing and nausea of a drug, but more a tugging and pulling of a normal body fixture, a dysfunctional part that's become a liability.

I enter a small room occupied by a forbidding dental chair where I'm surrounded by the instruments of torment. The occupants are wearing the suspicious white coats, and the glaring sterile apparatus is a reminder of ugly scenes.

I ascend the platform of the imposing dental chair and bury myself in its claustrophobic interior. The dentist asks, "Where does it hurt?"

I open my mouth wide and indicate the tooth with my finger. The dentist concurs that the tooth is decayed. The examination completed, I close my mouth and wait.

"Now open your mouth wide." I obey, observing there is no extension drill overhead. This is not a clinic for fillings. Grasping the arms of the chair tightly, I brace myself for the wrenching pain to come. How long must I hold myself in readiness?

"You may get down now," the dentist says.

"But aren't you going to take out my tooth?"

"It's already out," he says.

I don't remember that he gave me a needle or rubbed something on my gums. It's possible I had become immune to pain, the previous pain having been so much worse. I wasn't expecting any pain except that of extraction. This is my first experience with freezing. It's a revelation for more reasons than one.

⟶

J'm feeling more relaxed and am able to think more rationally, without fear. I tell my ward matron I would prefer to work in the dining room. The next morning I'm transferred from the factory. We don't use soap for washing dishes, just hot water. Cutlery is washed last. We also scrub the hardwood floor in the dining room with large pieces of yellow lye soap. "Haven't you ever scrubbed a floor before?" my fellow worker asks as she shows me how to make a wide soapy sweep.

A girl passes by with a tray of leftover toast from the staff dining room. I manage to grab a half slice. Miss Allison comes over and speaks to me. "You're looking much brighter," she says. I don't answer. She has been an aide to my humiliation and I don't like her.

It's unlikely she told anyone that Dr. Guest hid me in the toilet. She undoubtedly relies on the doctor's recommendation for future work. Still, it must have affected the doctor to show fear to an underling. It's an intimation that the doctor has deviated from accepted medical practice.

*C*HAPTER 11

*G*rey wool has been brought in, the first tangible indication a war is going on. Noon recreation, which used to take place in the wards, has been replaced with knitting garments in the dining room for the army. Also, times when girls would silently be consigned to their cells are now spent knitting in the general population. There's no segregation of first and repeat offenders. Only the women in for keeping a bawdy house are excluded.

My nursery duties having ended, I now join in. Some of the women know how to knit socks and balaclavas. I learn to knit a scarf.

This is the first time since the cool weather set in that we are all able to sit around and engage in conversation. The girls look sallow and pasty-faced from being indoors. I know no one has been out in the yard, probably because donning coats, footwear, and scarves would create supervisory and time problems. We have to be back at work on time. Furthermore, wearing our own coats and winter clothing might remind us of our own identities and make us less manageable.

Because we now mix together during these knitting sessions, I see and talk to the odd Belmont girl. I don't see the young woman who was a ward of the Children' Aid Society. I had asked her, "What's it like being a ward of the Children's Aid Society?"

"Tough," she replied.

She must be twenty-one years old by now and free from their supervision. Perhaps she's been released. I wonder why anyone would be a ward of the Children's Aid to twenty-one.

I'm surprised to see the auburn-haired minister's daughter here. I thought her father would have gotten her out. What would it be like if someone knew his daughter was in this disreputable place? It's unlikely members of her father's parish know his daughter is in an institution. Being incarcerated in the Mercer Reformatory would be even more humiliating for her father than having his daughter at the Belmont. If known, the family disgrace might affect his position in the ministry. I'm sure my being here is not known by anyone in Saint John. In the Good Shepherd's Home, it's said that the girls are given fictitious names when they enter. This would prevent the family name from being stigmatized by association with someone who had been imprisoned. This also makes it more difficult for inmates to contact one another when released. In both the Belmont Home and the Mercer Reformatory, our real names are used.

Any information about the world beyond these walls is rare. The information is generally from a visiting relative about personal things.

A Belmont girl comes over and confides, "Maria's brother came to visit her." We know that Maria is in for incest with him but he's family and so is entitled to visit.

I hear Jamie talking to another girl. Jamie has straight fair hair cut close like a boy. She doesn't appear to be more than twelve years old. She looks and talks like a little boy with a dress on. At the Belmont, I was told they were trying to keep Jamie apart from another girl who was sexually attracted to her. That would be no problem in the Mercer. They'd be separated in the same way I had been separated from the Belmont girls in my ward and at my table in the dining room. A girl could be put in a different workplace. Jamie never talks to me, probably because I was pregnant; she's too young to relate to anything like that. Right now she's talking excitedly to a girl sitting beside me, her eyes wide with fear. "We're going to have our spinals next week, the nurse said so." The girl answers in a barely audible tone; it's hardly a matter she wants to advertise. This is the first time I learn that Jamie has syphilis. It's inconceivable that this child has had sexual relations and a fateful encounter has given her syphilis, a disease said to take about two years to cure. Later I will see Jamie lying immobile in a cell.

⟶

*J*t's Saturday afternoon and rather than being quietly confined to our cells, we're busy doing our volunteer work, knitting and chatting. I spot Pearl, the mother who bathes the babies, sitting with another girl I don't know. From their demeanour I imagine the other girl might be a new mother. They're obviously not needed in the nursery and are sitting, heads bent, knitting and purling. I push past the crowded tables and lower myself into an empty chair beside them. I see that

Pearl is knitting a pair of socks. The other girl, probably a beginner like myself, is tackling a scarf. Pearl looks up. She eyes me uncertainly before speaking. We haven't seen each other since I was expelled from the nursery.

"Oh hello," she says, not knowing what response (sympathetic or otherwise) she should extend.

The circumstances of my departure from the nursery engender an uneasy feeling. What can one say in the brutal atmosphere of the Mercer where each person is obsessed with her own personal trauma?

I'm not put off and ask pointedly, "Do you know why my baby was sent to the hospital?"

The two women glance at each other. The new girl lowers her eyes and starts counting stitches. Pearl, who has a brood of her own, speaks. I assume she's not acquainted with the subtleties of avoidance.

"Don't say that I told you," Pearl says stealthily. "If you make any trouble I'll be blamed."

"No, I won't say anything, I promise."

"Well, I was bathing your baby and saw that his rash was getting worse. I had reported it to Miss Allison before but she didn't think it was serious. This time I told Miss McGrath. I was sure your baby had a fever. I have five of my own you know."

"Yes, I know."

"Nurse McGrath said I was not to put the baby on the porch but to put him in the crib in our cell. Not long afterwards, Dr. Bromley came in. I don't know where Dr. Hills was."

"Who's Dr. Bromley? How do you know it was him?"

"I saw him at 999."

"At 999! Why would a doctor from an insane asylum be brought in?"

"I don't know, and it's not an insane asylum, it's a mental hospital," says Pearl defensively. "My husband put me there for assessment but he had to let me out because there wasn't anything wrong with me. I was there for thirty days and I didn't get a shock treatment either."

Pearl looks apprehensively at the girl beside her who is still holding her head down. I know she feels uncomfortable letting it be known she was in 999.

"Is Dr. Bromley a psychiatrist?" I ask.

"I don't know. I think he's got something to do with fever machines."

"Dr. Bromley told Miss McGrath to give your baby some aspirin for his fever and a dressing for his ears and calamine lotion for his skin. Then he said loudly, 'I'm sending this baby to the Hospital for Sick Children.'"

"Miss Allison was there too. She glared at me with a warning expression like I shouldn't say anything. I know it was on the tip of her tongue but she didn't dare. She knows that gossip spreads like wildfire here and anything she said would add fuel to the fire. Dr. Bromley probably didn't know he should keep his voice down in a place like this. We aren't exactly mental patients to be completely ignored."

My impression of Pearl as placid, slow, and of no account changes. Her acute observations and her willingness to defy authority by telling me this surprises me. In this submissive and impersonal atmosphere where matrons never smile, Pearl is expressing sympathy. Usually, one's own pain diminishes the despair of others. But Pearl's bravery may be more than that. Perhaps the sexual demands of her husband had aroused her to commit a terrible act of violence. She may have crossed the line of tolerance and acquired a smoldering anger and resistance to authority. Maybe that's why she's here.

—

As we now mingle unimpeded in the dining room to knit items for the military, the difference in ages tends to manifest itself. There's the feeling that the older women don't want anything to do with the younger ones; similarly the younger ones search out one another.

Having seen some older girls strutting past with an air of privilege and entering the staff dining room or kitchen that are off-limits to others, I have the vague idea that they may have more information on the goings on in the Mercer or even the outside. I know that a lot of them are in for vagrancy or drunkenness. Many are repeaters, beyond rehabilitation from a judge's point of view, therefore likely to have shorter sentences. The younger girls transferred from a home, usually first-time offenders, have longer sentences. The older girls have little reason to try to escape. Also, they're experienced workers and the matrons don't have to watch them. That's probably why they get to work in food preparation.

I dare to install myself at a table with older women. I turn my chair sideways and keep my eyes affixed on my knitting.

A skinny woman with taut wrinkled skin is talking. "The last time they picked me up was in the women's beer parlour on Jarvis Street. I wasn't causing any trouble, just a little soused," she laughs.

"I know May, but the trouble with you is you're always getting into an argument with somebody."

"No I don't, Olive. I was minding my own business when the cops walked in. I was sitting with this guy who was standing outside the hotel. I brought him in with me."

"So he'd pay for the drinks," says Olive, a heavy woman with a moon-shaped face whose countenance reflects all the wisdom of an owl.

"The cops suspected I picked him up," says May.

"So right off they figured you were a prostitute," Olive retorts.

"Of course they all know me, that I like to take a drink." Coupled with the injury of her arrest, May exhibits a certain pride. She's on a first-name basis with the police.

"The guys are always sneaking over from the men's side—they don't have to wait outside for a woman to accompany them," says Olive adamantly.

"Some church people are trying to close down women's beer parlours," says May with an air of injustice.

"Who sentenced you?" Olive asks pointedly.

"Judge Browne," answers May. "I tried to explain that yes, I'd been drinking but I wasn't causing a disturbance. I pleaded not guilty but Judge Browne won't give anyone a chance to say anything."

"He barked at me," exclaimed May. "'Three months—next case.' Just like that! I wouldn't have expected to get more than thirty days."

"Anyone who's suspected of having VD is sent here whether they have it or not," says Olive. "She can be kept over her time and prevented from going out on parole."

"That's nothing to do with me," comes May's retort.

"I didn't say it had anything to do with you, I'm just saying," says Olive.

"They have to be charged with vagrancy," May responds.

"If they're on a roundup looking for diseased women, it doesn't matter what charges a girl is arrested under, even if the case can't be proved. Once a girl walks into the jail she gets examined and if the doctor isn't satisfied you're sent to the Mercer." Olive extends her fleshy arm and slices downward to emphasize her conviction. The movement causes her to tip her chair and she readjusts her broad hips.

"Well, there's lots of free clinics around, why don't they send them there?" May asks without expecting an answer.

"I don't know," Olive seems philosophical. "Maybe they need a lot of women to work in the laundry."

Olive points to one of the inmates and says, "Some of those Belmont girls they brought in are getting kind of mouthy. They looked like a bunch of scared bunnies when they first came in. You weren't here at the time May."

"I'll bet they've learned a lot since then," says May.

"Learning to be bitchy," says Olive, her double skin forming into deep folds. "Wait until they get out."

"Yeah, wait until they get out," May repeats.

"The first time I came into this hell hole," says Olive, "oh, it must have been more than ten years ago—no it was longer than that—well fourteen girls came down from Timmons. I think they were from a home. Anyway I thought that was a lot. But when I saw all the Belmont girls coming into the dining room I wondered, what the hell is going on! We twisted our necks trying to see the new girls in their granny dresses. A couple of matrons were pointing out seats at first-offender tables; they had to be separated from each other to prevent talking. They looked awfully young. A couple of them were pregnant."

"It's the young ones who have all the diseases," asserts Olive.

"How do you know they're sick?" asks May.

"Well, I don't know but it seems like the young ones who come in are always put on treatment," Olive says knowingly.

"Well, they're the ones most likely to attract men," says May.

"Yeah, and especially now with the war on, the soldiers have to be protected," Olive insists.

I adjust my chair, which had been placed with its back to the table. The movement brings attention to my presence. The women look at me suspiciously—no informers are welcome.

"Aren't you one of the girls they brought over from the Belmont Home?" Olive asks.

"Yes."

"You were pregnant when you came in, weren't you?"

"Yes, that's right."

"I thought so. Why aren't you upstairs taking care of your baby?"

"He was taken to the hospital."

There is a knowing look between the women. Probably everyone in the place knew about the Chinese baby that was taken to hospital. It was enough to disarm them. Anyone in my position would hardly be judgmental.

I resume my knitting and try to remain unobtrusive. I find their earthy conversation more interesting than that of more cautious young women and I don't want to move.

They resume their conversation. "One of the girls with syphilis told me she was taking treatments at St. Michael's Clinic when she got picked up for vagrancy, the night-walking section of the act. She says syphilis isn't contagious after a few months of treatment. She said it's no wonder girls beg the magistrate not to send them to the Mercer—she says she's being jabbed with a blunt needle in the buttock and she's sure the doctor here is using something really strong in the injections. If they did that at St. Mike's, no one would come back. I don't see her in the dining room today. Maybe she's sick in her cell—she says the side effects are awful: headaches and stomach cramps and some girls break out in a rash."

"This place is a bloody hospital!" Olive says vehemently. "It's a house of horrors! I was in Women's Court once when a woman begged the magistrate to give her a longer sentence and send her to Kingston Pen. He did, and she was smiling when they took her away."

A grey-haired woman approaches the table. She's carrying a large ball of coarse grey wool and a bulky unfinished garment.

"Hi Iris, what're you doing? knitting a horse blanket? Who do you think's going to wear it?"

May interrupts, "When are you getting your divorce Iris?"

"I'm not getting it—the bastard has moved away and I don't know what part of the country he's gone to. The law says I have to sue for divorce in my husband's domicile, the province where he lives. Anyway, my time's up next week so I'm getting out."

"Oh, you're leaving us, isn't that a shame." Olive smirks.

Iris lowers her voice to a whisper. "Do you know what happened to Bonnie? She made me swear not to tell anyone, so promise me you won't say anything."

"Not a word," says May earnestly. Olive nods in assent.

"Well, Bonnie said that a report went in that she had gonorrhea and her husband—he's in Guelph Reformatory—well he was examined as her contact. And he's really mad, says he doesn't have it, and that she was unfaithful. But she says she wasn't."

"So what's going to happen?" asks May. "Is that grounds for a divorce?"

"I don't know but Bonnie is fuming," says Iris. Having unburdened herself, she closes her eyes.

Then remembering, she adds, "The men at Guelph are allowed to smoke."

"Yes, I know," says Olive indignantly, "and they have toilets in their cells instead of stinking buckets."

Olive now submits her startling tidbit that she has been holding back. "A girl set fire to her cell last night," she says coolly.

"How do you know?" asks Iris.

"The girl who mops the floor in the infirmary told me. They brought her in with smoke inhalation but she wasn't so bad so they didn't keep her there. She's not in the infirmary any more and we think they put her in a punishment cell in the basement."

"Then they'll increase her sentence and send her to Kingston Pen," says May.

"Have you ever been in a punishment cell?" Olive directs her question to May.

"Not yet," says May, pursing her lips and shaking her thin mop of hair.

"I remember when you and me were both in." says Olive. "Oh about two years ago. I heard you talk back to a matron and I thought, Oh my God! She's in for it now! I've never been down in the basement cells but I know someone who was. She said it was the same size as our cells, but there was no mattress on the spring, and no light. She said she got three jam sandwiches a day and a meal every three days."[1]

"Just sit there and think what a jackass she was for being there," says May.

"Has anyone heard who the girl was that was in the clinic with Dr. Guest before the doctor left?" asks Iris.

"No, but everyone's talking about it. If anyone knows her name I haven't heard it but I have my own ideas about that." Olive's inner reflection fails to provoke curiosity.

"Whoever it was must have died because Dr. Guest hasn't come back," says May.

Just then the bell rings. The knitting is put aside, and the girls assemble in file and are directed to their cells.

Although many of us may visit the doctor regularly, no one talks about it. The type of medical procedure we undergo is degrading and none of us knows what the other endures. Only the older women are unafraid to use medical words with their ominous meanings.

⸺

*I*t doesn't take long via the grapevine to learn that Dr. Hills is from another reformatory, the Burwash Industrial Farm. He was hired on at Burwash when a physician was let go for medically abusing prisoners three years ago. Now he's taking over from Dr. Guest. I can't help wondering if Dr. Hills is being used to pull chestnuts out of the fire.

I wonder if the girl who set fire to her cell was attempting suicide. No doubt she'll be charged with damaging prison property. I recall the Native girl descending the steps with tears in her eyes. It was syphilis treatment day and I believe she was coming from the doctor's. I see the girl with epilepsy who sat next to me in the dining room. She has gained weight and lost her beauty. I think it's because of the high starch content in the food. I recognize the emaciated woman I had seen in the window from the yard, a small woman, perhaps in her forties. She looks quite human in her regular Mercer uniform.

There's a jolly buxom girl from the Belmont Home in my ward now. Her personality remains unchanged. She's laughing and telling us how she corseted herself to hide her pregnancy from her parents. "When I went to the hospital my parents thought I had appendicitis."

Her parents adopted her baby and they visit her regularly with her three-year-old daughter.

⸺

*T*he girl in the next cell to mine has made me a confidante. Hélène has dark hair and south European features like mine. Her parents, who are Italian, have disowned her.

"A woman from the Children's Aid came to see me," she says. "They wanted to know how I was going to take care of my daughter when I got out, if I had made any arrangements."

"How old is your baby?" I enquire.

"She's just fourteen months," she answers, becoming distracted by emotion.

"What did you tell the Children's Aid woman?"

"I said I wouldn't be getting out for awhile yet."

"How can you make arrangements in here?" I exclaim.

"I know! The social worker said they wanted to know my plans—that my baby would be better off with a proper family, that with me she'll suffer the stigma of being born illegitimate. It might be better to put her up for adoption. Has anyone been to see you?" she asks me.

"No," I say. It occurs to me that my baby would never be adoptable, not only because he's sick but because of his mixed race.

"But you might get married and that would solve everything," I say.

"Yes, I would get married if I could have a home for my baby but they're not prepared to wait, that's the trouble. What really worries me is that while I'm in here, the Children's Aid are taking care of my daughter and I don't know how I'm going to get her back. They'll say I'm an unfit mother because I was in the Mercer."

Unfit mother! The thought stuns me. Could her vagrancy charge be for not giving a proper account of herself, or for being a night walker, a prostitute? That would seal her fate.

"Perhaps you'll be able to find a job," I say.

"Maybe, but I'm not experienced at anything," she says ruefully. Hélène turns to me. "Tell me your address and I'll look you up when I get out."

Getting out isn't something I think about, but I answer, "You can find me through my mother's name in the telephone book." I spell out my last name. "But I'd better tell you, my boyfriend is Chinese."

"I know" she says. "Somebody told me your baby was taken to hospital. Are you going to marry the baby's father?"

"Yes," I say. "I will."

—

"*D*o you remember me? You sat beside me at my table when you first came in. You thought you'd be in for only thirty days." I address the woman I come across during knitting time in the dining room.

"Yes, I remember," says the slightly older woman. "That was quite a long time ago. You were pregnant."

"Yes." There's no mention of the baby. The subject is best overlooked. She probably doesn't know there's a nursery here and would think that the baby was born in the Mercer, likely apprehended by the Children's Aid.

"I thought you'd moved to another table but I looked around and couldn't see you," I say.

"I was over at 999," she says frankly.

"At 999—what were you doing there? Did the psychiatrist send you over?" I have intense curiosity.

"No, it wasn't that, it was something else. I don't exactly want to talk about it."

"I'm sorry, I didn't mean to be nosy. But I never thought a girl would go to a mental hospital and then come back to the Mercer."

"Well, I'll tell you but I don't want it to get around. It's private. You're the only one who noticed I was gone."

There's a feeling of trust between us. Perhaps she thinks I've suffered by having my baby taken away at birth. Feeling set apart, I'm sympathetic to anyone who has a secret.

"They put me in the Black Maria—didn't tell me where we were going. I thought they might be taking me back to court to grant my release. Instead I was driven to the Ontario Mental Hospital a few blocks away. That same day I saw the doctor. While I was standing there, he said to the nurse, 'This is another asymptomatic case sent over from the Mercer. This girl is to be given fever therapy.'"

"What do they mean by asymptomatic?"

"The nurse said my spinal fluid was suspicious. They're giving me fever treatment as a preventative measure against syphilis. The nurse said fever is also used for gonorrhea in women where diagnosis is difficult and for other diseases like cancer. Anyway, I had to get into this fever machine. It's a wooden box about six feet long with an opening at the top. I kept on my white hospital clothes and the nurse helped me to step onto the mattress. Then she closed the lid, leaving only my head out."

"It sounds awful!" I am comparing her climbing into the fever cabinet with myself climbing onto the clinic table.

"They keep you in there for six or seven hours. I could feel the sweat dribbling down. Because it takes so long, different people in white coats kept coming round checking the thermometer so it wouldn't go too high. I was always scared when they walked away, that no one would be watching. The machine can get too hot."

"How high is it supposed to go?"

"It's not supposed to go higher than 106 degrees. Sometimes, when I said it was too hot, the operator would open up the sliding door on the side for a couple of minutes to cool me off. They would give me salt water every so often. I kept drifting in and out of sleep. I felt so weak when I got out I could hardly stand up."

"How long were you in 999?"

"Almost two months with a treatment every week. There were other women there taking treatments, one with epilepsy. Someone said it's used for arthritis too. Some patients got malaria injections to raise their temperatures but thank goodness I didn't get that!"

"They told my sister when she came to see me at the Mercer that I wasn't available. She wasn't told why—they're not allowed to tell relatives that a girl has VD. Later I told my sister I had pneumonia and was in the infirmary. Don't tell anyone what happened."

"I won't say anything," I affirm.

"I know you won't."

I contemplate what it would be like for someone who suffers from claustrophobia to lie in a fever machine. I try not to visualize the ordeal.

This will be the last time I see her. She must have gotten out. This cheers me up, and I promise myself that some day I'll look up Mabel Majurski.

—

*W*e're standing around in the corridor outside our cells. Some of the girls have retired to their small units. The matron will be coming along any time to lock us in.

A girl is talking to several others. "My husband visited me and told me that it's called sulphanilamide. He says they're calling it a miracle drug."

"Sulphanilamide? I've never heard of it," Laura says flatly.

She leans against a cell door, crosses her arms, and lowers her languid dark eyes. To be on the good side of Laura is to avoid criticism.

Barbara, freckled and earnest, feels obliged to retain her credibility. "Well, the reason you didn't hear about it is because it's something new—they're just starting to use it. They're using it for all sorts of things; it cures everything fast."

"I don't believe there's such a thing as a wonder drug," Laura says with an air of dismissal.

The girls turn away.

"My husband says he's going to join the army," Barbara says proudly. There's a renewal of interest.

"He has to be accepted first," Laura remarks.

A French-Canadian girl with a decided accent is talking about the weird sexual request of a male friend. It's incredible! We all laugh. I feel myself laughing for the first time since my arrest.

She says emphatically, "Eet's true, eet's true."

The circumstances of my baby being taken to hospital have unnerved me but to share my misery with other inmates would be improper. I fail to mention it to a girl who has recently come into my ward. Whatever she's learned about me is never discussed. We've become friendly and tend to seek out a corner of the ward where we can't be heard. She believes she's more refined than the others—she's here by mistake and not for an offence. She tells me I'm different, quiet and ladylike.

"It's not right!" she says angrily. "I was in jail on remand. My lawyer said I was sure to get off because I wasn't guilty. It was late at night when I got off from my waitress job and was walking home when a policeman arrested me for vagrancy. When the magistrate in the women's police court said 'charge withdrawn' I was so relieved. Then a man from the health department stood up and said, 'There's a holding order for this woman.' In a flash, my lawyer stood up and said, 'I would request of the court that my client go to her own doctor for examination.' But the judge refused."

"What's a holding order?" I ask.

"It's when the jail doctor says you have vd. By law the doctor only has to be suspicious. My lawyer said it wouldn't do any good to try to appeal the decision. Then I got sent here."

"How long will you have to stay in for?" I ask. It's the one question that's not considered intrusive. It isn't a good idea to ask a girl what she's in for but everyone wants to tell the length of her sentence. "My lawyer says until the Mercer doctor says I'm cured or decides to let me out—not more than a couple of months I hope. My lawyer says he's doing his best."

CHAPTER 12

"*C*ome with me," says the matron. I follow her for some distance toward the west wing of the building. We're distancing ourselves from the other inmates and as we approach a door she says, "You're going home."

I'm not immediately overcome with joy. The matron's probably disappointed. My response doesn't meet her expectations. I can't grasp the significance of her words. How is it that I'm being released so early? It's March 1, 1940. Even with good time and without being penalized for my escape, it's a month too soon. But it's not that. I can't find a happy emotional response. It isn't part of my newly developed approach to life.

I enter a storage area where my suitcase is retrieved and change into my own clothes. They're the same ones I was wearing when taken to the courthouse. It's not until I feel the silk stockings on my legs and put on my Cuban-heeled shoes that I realize I'm leaving. I'm given six dollars, less than I would have expected. I try to add up the six cents a day but realize I wasn't always working. There was the time I spent in solitary and in the hospital having my baby and on treatment days in my cell.

My mother is in the waiting room, all smiles. With my baby in hospital there are no complications. Had my son been healthy, she would have been hard-pressed to take me with the baby into her home. My brother's animosities about race would have made home life difficult at best. Yet I think she would have done it rather than have social workers scavenging about looking for the father to provide for the baby's maintenance. She is undoubtedly pleased that fate intervened and the problem of accommodating her daughter with her baby has evaporated. As for the Mercer authorities, my release is a godsend to them. Otherwise, and had the hospital discharged my baby, there would have been difficulties. The Mercer would not want to accommodate a convalescent baby and probably would have placed him in a foster home. Social workers from the Infants' Home would have made inquiries. They would contact the hospital for a detailed account of all circumstances surrounding my baby's illness. I suspect this is a question the Mercer authorities don't want to be asked. I learn later that Dr. Bromley didn't even leave his name with the Hospital for Sick Children when my baby was admitted.

I greet my mother with the same non-joyous attitude I exhibited to the matron. My mother looks disappointed. She does not recognize that my spontaneity is blighted. She wants me to share the same excitement that this day means to her. She wants to keep her daughter.

I carry my suitcase as we descend the steps and walk the long distance to the gates of the institution. We're on the street a short distance from the place, walking towards my mother's car, when it strikes me. I say, "Wait a minute," put down my suitcase, and take a long look at the Mercer Reformatory. It's still bathed in shade but the sun is shining on the trees and grass surrounding the building.

I need to see the place where part of my life is buried and then expel it from mind. My mother finds this farewell behaviour interesting. She smiles with satisfaction. I've revealed some feeling. She knows I'm recognizing my freedom and this day as a landmark in my life.

My mother drives me home and we ascend the steps of her new little house in that part of Toronto called Cabbagetown. She hovers about me, anxious that I should not go out. But there's nothing she can do when I say, "I'm going downtown for awhile." It's ironic that my mother, who tried to exert so much control over me, has lost it entirely.

I've heard nothing about my baby since he went to hospital. I prefer not to let my mother hear me enquiring about him. My first stop is at a pay phone. I call the Hospital for Sick Children. They tell me my son is in the preventorium, a section attached to the hospital. Satisfied in knowing where he is, I head for the Commodore Café on Yonge Street where my boyfriend used to work. Without hesitation I'm told of his new workplace in Barrie. It's about sixty miles from Toronto. I have the six dollars from the Mercer, more than enough for a return ticket by bus.

As I board the bus I have every confidence that my fiancé and I will resume the life we knew. There's an emotional stability about him that I also see in his friends from China. I expect it was this that was part of my attraction to him. Although I suffered physical pain at the Mercer, I never felt mentally insecure about Harry. I know that he will accept our son.

I feel restored as I travel towards my destination. I never entertained the thought of losing Harry. My security is assured by the fact of his culture as well as our love. The legal isolation of Chinese men from female companionship ensures that I will always be taken care of. He's attractive but I don't dream there's any competition. I recall his self-discipline. I can't be wrong.

I see him through the window at the designated restaurant. He's serving customers. Now I remember what entrances me about him— it's the way he moves his body.

I walk into the restaurant. We laugh at the sight of each other. We don't embrace each other in public. We're both too conservative for that. Our love is in our eyes and expression. We renew our unspoken vows as if I had never been gone.

Assuming he thought I'd been living with my father in Saint John, I tell him I've been in a reformatory and had a baby. My fiancé laughs with delight at news of the baby and tells his co-workers he has a son. It's decided he will come to Toronto to see the baby the following day.

We stand outside a window and view our baby among a number of others, all lying in separate cribs. He's easy to recognize, being the only Asian baby there. His eyes are open, his face flushed and arms down in a white hospital tunic. We don't realize he's in straitjacket. Harry laughs and says, "He has one eye larger than the other just like me." We're optimistic. Our main concern is to bring our child home.

We're still in the midst of the Depression. Although it's 1940 and the war has been going on for months, it has not yet generated a surplus of jobs. It's essential that Harry obtain work in Toronto where accommodation can more readily be found for our family.

In the meantime I'm anxious to get out of my mother's house. I telephone an ad under "Domestic Help Wanted" and am hired the same day. Domestic positions have been available throughout the Depression. The ads offering the best salaries are for experienced cooks from Scandinavian countries.

My monthly employment is with a middle-aged couple with a ten-year-old boy. The large house is in an exclusive residential district. My duties consist of preparing breakfast, making beds, vacuuming carpets throughout, including the spiral staircase, dusting, scrubbing three bathrooms, washing dishes, and polishing silver. My day finishes at eight o'clock when I retire. Wednesday after two o'clock is my day off.

The boy goes to school. When he brings home a classmate, he asks me to remove his boots and refers to me as the maid.

I assume that the couple have only recently got the house, because when the boy mentions his former neighbourhood, his mother says, "shush."

I don't get the same food as my employers and have to procure what I can. I'm afraid to ask where or what is available. The woman prepares the meals, which they eat quietly in the den. I occasionally steal a homemade bun from a tray and hope it won't be missed. My employer says, "You can fry an egg for dinner." I crack the egg into a frying pan that isn't hot enough and it becomes messy. She says, "Haven't you ever fried an egg before?"

It's decided I should wear a uniform and she has obtained two designs for approval. "Which pattern do you like?" she asks. One of the patterns is the same blue and white pinstripe worn at the Mercer.

I point to the plain blue.

"I like the other one better," she says, keeping two in the pinstripe design. "I'll send the others back."

I want to leave but because I'm hired by the month, I believe I may not receive any pay. There's no one ever to talk to. I don't feel privileged to use the telephone and can't even contemplate a long distance call to Harry.

One day she asks me, "My husband says you seem to be dragging your feet. Is there anything wrong?"

"I'm not feeling well," I say. I tell her I have a baby in the hospital.

"Maybe you're pregnant again," she says.

She talks quietly to her husband and returns. "I won't be needing you anymore, but I'm letting you take the uniforms with you—they're not likely to fit anyone else. They cost one dollar each and I'm deducting it from your wages."

Wages are eighteen dollars a month but I'm relieved to get eight for my half month's work. Her husband drives me back to my mother's where he had previously picked me up.

—

*D*ue to a chest cold I'm visiting my family doctor. He puts his fingers to the sides of my throat and says, "I don't know why you never gain weight—perhaps it's your glands." It's an opportunity for me to enquire about my medical experience at the Mercer.

"There's no such thing as gonorrhea warts," he says bluntly. "But cancer studies on the wart virus have been going on for years. Cancer is a terrible disease, there's no cure." He sounds bitter.

His answer extends no sympathy towards me. I'm not a guinea pig for the wart virus, I think angrily. He makes no further comment, focuses his attention on writing a prescription, and then brusquely terminates the visit. My anger propels me to visit a medical library. I find that genital warts are called human papilloma virus. It can be kept in a refrigerator and inoculated into the skin of volunteers. It can be tested only on humans because it is not transferable to animals, thus severely restricting research.

—

*H*arry has found a job in Toronto and rented a room and we've moved in together. The room is on the second floor of a house rented by a Chinese man and his French-Canadian wife on Gerrard Street, several blocks from Chinatown. Water is available from the bathroom on the same floor and there's a small balcony overlooking the street. We buy a bed and dresser and put our pots into wooden apple crates. For cooking we have a single-burner hot plate.

I say, "We'd better get married right away as I might be arrested again. I'm not twenty-one yet."

Harry gets time off from the restaurant in the afternoon and, together with Margaret (whom I went to Church Street School with), and a Chinese friend of Harry's, we assemble at a church where the Protestant Chinese minister conducts the marriage ceremony in English. We sign a register, and afterwards Harry goes back to work and we all leave. The next day we go to a government registry office and have our son's name changed to that of his father.

—

*T*he day has come to pick up our baby. He's been in hospital for five months and we still don't know why.

Our son is passed into my arms, wrapped in a blanket by a nurse who generously supplies me with some cotton baby clothes. I'm appalled to find that the skin on his face is red and scaly. The nurse tells me the baby must be washed only with olive oil, no water, and that he cannot wear wool. She further advises he must be given canned milk and pro-vides me with a black tar ointment for his skin. I'm instructed to bring him to the hospital clinic in a week.

We take him home and put him in a basket. I now find he has big scabs on his head and that the skin disease extends over his whole body. Immediately we realize he will scratch himself to pieces if we don't bind his hands, so I tie each one with rags, securing them to the sides of the basket. He moves his head back and forth to get relief from the itching. The tar ointment gets onto his clothes. No matter how much I wash them they look dirty.

A public health nurse visits. She's a slight, well-groomed woman with bobbed hair. I imagine she got my name from the hospital. Does she know other things about me? That my baby was sent to hospital from the Mercer? She can't be a nurse, for she hasn't touched my baby. Still I know she's observing the details: my baby's inflamed skin with dabs of black ointment. Perhaps she's a social worker. They're required to follow up on single mothers released from the reformatory. I've been traced here by someone.

The woman remains standing near the open door despite my invi-tation to come in. I expect my small space is not too inviting.

I dare to ask, "You know I was in the Mercer?"

"Yes," she replies.

She avoids any reference to my shoddy past and says in reference to my baby, "Why you're nothing but a child yourself."

I look young because I weigh about a hundred pounds. The visitor has little to say about how I should care for my baby.

I attend the hospital clinic as instructed. "What's wrong with my baby?" I ask the physician on duty.

"He has a bad case of eczema," he says.

"What caused it?" I ask, wondering if it hadn't been for the illness and meals I missed at the Mercer, things might have been different.

"It's hereditary," he says.

My husband is proud of having a baby, and brings a friend to see his son. He does that once and never again. The baby was unclothed and I was washing him with olive oil.

I visit the clinic each week and each time it's a different doctor. They always try to change the baby's milk formula. I'm advised to buy an expensive powdered milk that we can ill afford. As instructed, I mix it with water and boil it for six hours. It's summer and our room is hot.

In the evening I sit on the balcony and hold the baby in my arms. I get a rash on my forearm where his head rests.

—

*M*y husband works every day until the early hours of the morning. He's off for a short time in the afternoon and I go out.

"What have you done?" I say when I return. "You know you're not supposed to give the baby a bath!" My husband looks perplexed. He has little faith in western medicine. The baby is crying.

Our landlady comes halfway up the stairs screaming about her electric bill, telling us we will have to get out. I have used the electric plate constantly, also lots of hot water in washing baby clothes. I'm guilty so don't answer.

—

*O*n this weekly visit to the hospital my baby is admitted. The public health nurse visits me and suggests I place my son in a foster home temporarily and pay his board. The foster parent is a children's nurse with a proper home. My husband is rarely home so I'm the spokesperson for the family. I agree with the public health nurse and convince my husband that we have no choice.

Caring for my child eased my loneliness but now I feel the full impact of my situation. There are no visitors. The Mercer psychiatrist was right. I'm ostracized.

I never speak of my prison experience to my husband. It could only bring despair that our child's illness is serious and not easily curable. I accept my husband's philosophy that our child was smitten by the hand of fate.

—

*I*t has been some months since I left the Mercer and I still haven't detached myself from the horrific experience. I keep feeling that we girls should not have been sent there. I go to see Miss Pollock at the Belmont Home—she's still there. The building has been changed; they made a lot of alterations. The iron grilles have been removed from all the windows and fire escapes extend to the ground. The inside is almost unrecognizable: there's a new stairway and a beautiful dining room. I'm surprised by the renovations, and ask Miss Pollock about them. She says, "The Belmont Home is being changed to a home for the elderly. It will be called Ewart House."

"I thought the home didn't have any money and couldn't afford to keep us?"

Miss Pollock responds to my brazen remark. "A gentleman donated a lot of money to enable us to make the change. The laundry at the Belmont Home couldn't compete with other laundries and the government wouldn't give the board any money to upgrade the equipment. Charitable donations for the girls had also fallen off and those for the other two aged homes on Belmont Street increased. You probably didn't know that the board was operating two homes for the aged besides the Belmont Home."

"No, I didn't know." As if that would make any difference! I continue my questions. "All the girls from the Belmont weren't transferred to the Mercer—were they let out?"

"No, eighteen of the older girls were kept behind. You know, some of the girls had been in the Belmont for years because they liked it here and didn't want to leave. Some of them are very old."

"How old?" I ask.

"About fifty to seventy years, I would guess. Some of the girls can remember when they helped care for the elderly residents in the homes for the aged, before they were sent to the Home for Incurables."[1]

"That must have been a long time ago."

"Yes, it could be as far back as 1918 or thereabouts, before you were born."

I don't ask if some of them are doing the laundry because it wouldn't be polite.

"I've heard that the Belmont Home was once a home for the feeble-minded. I guess if I'd been in the home a few years ago I'd be looked on as feeble-minded."

Confronted by a resentful ex-inmate, Miss Pollock retains her moderate posture. "The Belmont Home hadn't been accepting feeble-minded girls for years—they were sent to The Haven. We had a certain reputation to maintain; we provided our girls with references and tried to place them in good homes as domestics if they were agreeable. Employers," she says firmly, "want a certain type of girl."

Miss Pollock continues. "'For the Feebleminded' hasn't been on the cover of our annual reports since 1931. The official name of the Belmont Home is 'The Toronto Industrial Refuge,' though even the judges don't know it. The home got its name because it's been on Belmont Street for so many years."

Miss Pollock extols the stability and dedication of the Belmont Home. "When the home first started we offered to help the girls live better lives. If they promised to stay for a year we would train them and provide them with clothing and references."

"Someone said the home was supposed to rehabilitate us."

"Yes, we tried to bring Christ to the girls," Miss Pollock replies. Even the kindest of people like Miss Pollock wants to feel benevolent on their own terms.

"Some of the girls were put on treatment by the doctor at the Mercer after they arrived," I say.

"I expect any treatment the girls got at the Mercer couldn't be for anything serious. Dr. Ayer's report stated that all the girls were in very excellent health."[2] Miss Pollock wavers for a moment. "The board anguished over what to do but they had no choice but to let the girls go." She seems to be apologizing.

$\mathcal{C}$HAPTER 13

$\mathcal{A}$ woman approaches me on the street. "I hear you were in the Mercer," she says. "Would you like to make some money?" I ignore her.

I go to a movie with a girlfriend. "My boyfriend says that I shouldn't go out with you—someone might think I go around with Chinese."

I'm working at Hunt's Ice Cream Parlour on Yonge Street below College when Dr. Guest walks in. My back is to her and I'm wearing my waitress uniform when she says, "I'm in a hurry." I turn around and face her. There's instant recognition but neither of us says hello. She orders a sandwich. A criminal thought passes my mind—if I only had some poison.

———

$\mathcal{T}$he time has arrived for me to look up Mabel Majurski. I wonder if she has recovered from her experience in 999. She's easily traced in the phone book; a relative advises she's in hospital. I spy her lying in bed in a public ward of the General Hospital. There are twenty beds, evenly divided, extending from opposite sides of a large white room. Each bed has white curtains that can be drawn when privacy is required by the doctor.

"We're not allowed to get out of bed," says Mabel, her pale face exaggerated by her dark brown shoulder-length hair. I don't know why I thought she was older in the Mercer. She's probably in her twenties. She points out the nurses who are wearing blue and white short-sleeved blouses crisscrossed in the back with full white skirts. On their heads are white caps.

They're nurses in training," says Mabel. "They give us bedpans and, if we're lucky, a back rub," says Mabel.

"I had an abortion," she says in a low voice. "It's against the law," she whispers. "I told the doctor I had a miscarriage. Some of the other women have had one too."

I look around at the faces of those women sitting up in their beds and try to guess which woman had a deliberate miscarriage. I know that abortions are illegal and merit a jail sentence.

"Two women came to my house and one of them did it," says Mabel. "I asked them, 'Are you sure it will work?' The women laughed and said, 'It will work all right.' I didn't see what she used but it felt like a needle—I moved and got a second jab in the wrong place. Of course it's hush hush. I don't even know their names—a friend sent them. I paid them forty dollars. I was bleeding and came to the hospital. An intern admitted me. I had my womb scraped yesterday and I should be going home in a few days."

She points to a woman a few beds down from her. "A doctor wheedled out of her that she'd done her own abortion. Since you come out and tell them they're obliged to write it down. That's her over there, and that's her husband visiting her. She has three children but they're not allowed in the ward."

I follow her eyes to see a rather large woman sitting up in bed, looking glum. She appears to be younger than her husband who is a short slightly built man with greying hair. He's sitting on a chair beside her bed.

Squinting her nose at her white cotton hospital attire, Mabel says, "If I hadn't had to come in so fast I would have brought a pretty nightgown to wear like some of the other women here."

There's no mention of the Mercer and I get the feeling that Mabel doesn't want to talk about old times. I wonder if I did the right thing in looking her up. She hasn't asked me any questions either.

Just then she reaches over and whispers, "Sometimes they wheel you out for examination. Students look us over. Sometimes the doctor will hide my face with a curtain, but sometimes they don't bother. It's very embarrassing—some of the guys are no older than me."

I'm lost for words. Mabel, seeing my expression, turns her head away to hide her feelings. Then she changes the subject. "I'm working as a waitress at the Statler Hotel. We serve beer and the tips are good. You might be able to get on there but you would have to lie about your age. You have to be twenty-one to serve beer."

"I don't have enough experience to work in a place like the Statler," I say, feeling it's generous of Mabel to suggest it.

She reaches into the drawer of her small hospital cabinet and retrieves a camera. "My boyfriend brought it to me on his last visit, to cheer me up he says. It's a Zeiss," she says proudly. "It's made in Germany. My boyfriend said, 'With the war going on it will be impossible to get anything like this.'"

I hold it in my palm, feel the weight, and touch the black leather texture. I've never seen anything quite as elegant. Everyone knows the best cameras and binoculars are made in Germany. Even my father never had a camera like this, only a square Kodak. Her boyfriend must be well off, probably an older man.

Mabel directs my attention to an extremely thin woman with stringy dark hair who lies under a rounded contraption that covers her abdomen. "It's a heat lamp," she explains. "One of the patients called out to her, 'If you don't gain any weight, your husband will think he's on a washboard,'" Mabel says laughing.

It strikes me that, for a girl who has been through hell in the fever machine, she's sure bounced back.

—

I answer a knock on the door and in walks Hélène, my next-door cellmate from the Mercer. She's beaming. "At last I found you!" she says, excited. "I phoned your mother and she said you were married and working as a waitress. Where's your baby?"

It's said peremptorily. Hélène has sat down at my table without looking at the surroundings, obviously unaware of anything but her having found me.

"He's still sick. I'm boarding him with a children's nurse." I know she's barely listening.

It's been a long time and it's obvious she's pregnant again. I'm afraid to ask about her daughter, probably over two years old by now.

"I don't know what to do," she says. "The Infant's Home still has my little girl. They want me to sign papers to give her up for adoption. I'm living with my boyfriend and because we're not married I can't have her. My boyfriend is married and his wife won't give him a divorce."

Her situation looks hopeless. Living with a married man out of wedlock poses all kinds of problems. She can't bring her daughter into a sinful environment. Even if her boyfriend is the father of her unborn child, after its birth she will be living in an unmarried union.

"Would it do any good if you were living somewhere else?" I ask.

"No, because I wouldn't have any means of support. No one is going to hire someone who's pregnant," she replies.

—

$\mathcal{A}$s the war escalates, the radio reports the transfer of occupants from schools, mental hospitals, and penal institutions. The buildings are needed to make room for military personnel. Government institutions are severely overcrowded. Having wholeheartedly given lands and buildings to the military, the premier now finds they won't accept prisoners into the army as was customary during the last war. "We will have to manage as best we can," he advises.

Patients from the newly built mental hospital at St. Thomas are being sent to the Langstaffe Prison Farm. I imagine them being placed in ugly cell blocks after being relocated only six months earlier in St. Thomas Hospital with its modern cafeteria. Did they or their relatives know they were being sent to the prison farm? Did the St. Thomas patients undergo the same experience as the Belmont girls—shock and far less accommodating quarters? They're being scheduled to work on the hundred-acre site. It's said that they want to do their bit for the war effort.

There's more jobs now. I picture all the girls I knew, now released, getting married to soldiers, starting new lives, and able to keep any babies they might bear. The women are "Rosie the Riveters" just as the men are "our brave lads in the forces." Even my mother has exchanged fortune telling for a job in a munitions factory.

By 1942 Canada Manpower had been set up and Selective Service cards issued to each person in order to mobilize the population toward jobs, particularly those essential to the wartime economy. To obtain employment, a person has to visit a Manpower office and speak to a clerk. There's a search of positions available and a phone call is made to the prospective employer.

Newspapers report a roundup of prostitutes. Radio and army reports assert that Canada is determined to keep her fighting men fit, that action seeks out and brings to justice those who, for personal gain, cater to men's weaknesses. "We must hold at bay the master saboteurs of the war effort. The will to banish this fifth column in our midst must encompass a concerted attack." A health magazine claims that the real menace is the growing number of "khaki kids" who hang around barracks and railway stations or go soldier hunting in dance halls. These are girls ranging from twelve to sixteen.

Newspapers report knitted articles donated by organizations for the welfare of soldiers. There's no mention of the scarves, sweaters, socks, and other garments knitted by Mercer women.

In the women's section of the newspapers are pictures of debutantes—marriageable young women at their coming-out parties and photographs of newlyweds, army officers, and brides with honeymoon destinations.

There's also news about the reformatory. The *Toronto Telegram* of January 11, 1943, reports: "Attempts Fail, Add Outsiders, Health Board." Apparently Dr. Bates and Dr. Guest have applied to the city for positions on the health board but their postings are not approved. A controversy is raging over whether women should be drinking with men in beer parlours. Dr. Guest has publicly stated, "Close up beer parlours where women sit down to drink."

The papers report on how powerful the Female Refuges Act is. There's a story in *Justice Weekly*, April 6, 1946, that claims there is "Nothing Wrong with Having Child, Children's Aid Ward Tells Bench." It describes how Eileen Hannigan, a fair and slender twenty-year-old ward of the Children's Aid, pregnant by her boyfriend, is brought into Women's Court. Like me, she insists she will get married if she is released but no effort is made to accommodate her wishes. She is sentenced under the Female Refuges Act to two years in the Mercer Reformatory. The act prevents a marriage of choice by a woman between the ages of eighteen and twenty-one without the permission of parents or guardians, even though the Marriage Act states that a woman can marry without restriction at eighteen years.

CHAPTER 14

*W*e rent a flat, buy some furniture, and bring our son home.
He's two years old, not yet walking, and still suffering
from the severe skin ailment, especially on his face. With the baby in a
carriage, I meet a girl from a former workplace.

She asks, "Where did you get the baby?"

When I say, "He's mine," she doesn't believe me.

An older woman smiles and says, "What a nice baby." Bless her.

My son gets an abscess behind his ear, and his leg has also become
infected. He is again taken into hospital.

I'm pregnant again and horrified. I haven't told my husband of my
Mercer ordeal. It would be too disparaging to the baby. If he connects
the baby's health to my imprisonment, he doesn't say anything. I tell
him I must have an abortion. Abortions are illegal, but my friend
Linda has contacts. She has found a bona fide doctor who will do it
for a hundred dollars. I don't have any money so have to contact my
father. He'll give me the money if I agree to leave Toronto and return
home.

My husband is opposed to the abortion but is unable to dissuade
me. He doesn't have the memories I sustain of my former painful pregnancy. These act on my mind as a denigration of my child, a form of
hopelessness that he will never be well. If we had a healthy child we
could have escaped to a cultural refuge. My son as a baby could have
learned the Chinese language, the key to cultural acceptance.

A decision had to be made. How to care for a new child when I
couldn't cope with my first? I go to the doctor's office one evening.
He's alone. Without anaesthetic, I endure the procedure. The results
are satisfactory.

I sell our furniture and give the money to my husband to save,
telling him I'll be coming back. I make arrangements with the Infants'

Home to look after Harry Junior. Each of us will contribute to our son's support. I know I'll be assuming my cashier's job in my father's theatre.

Harry confesses he gambled and lost our savings. I feel angry but don't express it. Did he think that good fortune would prevent me from leaving? Perhaps. I could have paid back my father and escaped my obligation. Good fortune might have alleviated the burden of help-lessness.

My brother is no longer in the house. My mother says, "I sent him to your father to put into business." She had encouraged his marriage to a girl from a poor province who rented the room upstairs next to my brother's.

It's Saturday and my mother is conducting her weekly poker game.

When Linda and I arrive, my mother says, beaming, "The girls are here." She gets up from the table where the game has already started so she can rearrange the chairs.

Sam, my mother's live-in boyfriend, raises his head from the game and without smiling conveys a feeling of satisfaction. Sam looks to be in his early fifties, about my mother's age, Canadian of Irish descent. His movements are deliberately slow, indicating an intel-lectual attitude towards inferiors, especially my mother. She bears his caustic remarks with good humour—she's the boss—it's her house. No one shows interest in my mother's failings. She smiles slightly. She's wearing a bright bandanna and sits solemnly, taking short puffs on a cigarette that burns quickly; she doesn't inhale. Mrs. Shroeder, the elderly other player, doesn't bother to acknowledge our presence. She continues to look at the table as if the game hadn't been inter-rupted. No one expects any change of expression from her nor does she generally speak at all.

We throw our nickels onto the table prior to each hand of cards. It's called the pot. My mother will take out some money to pay for the cof-fee and sandwiches. I remember what she told me at the Mercer, that Mrs. Shroeder had to be watched lest she take money out of the pot when supposedly putting it in.

We're playing seven-card poker with deuces wild. For starters we all throw a nickel into the centre of the table. Sam looks at his hand and throws in a dime. To stay in the game we all toss in our dimes. The money clinks quietly onto the soft tablecloth. On the seventh card Sam raises the ante twenty-five cents. The rest of us have dropped out. Mrs. Shroeder puts in her money, then opens her hand to reveal three sixes. Whatever cards Sam has we never know but he can't beat three sixes. Mrs. Shroeder extends her scrawny arms to draw in the booty, mostly dimes.

The arrival of Tony, the Italian shoemaker, comes with a sharp draught from the door and the air of a pleasure seeker. Despite a limp, which is of no importance, his smiles, booming voice, and personality bring relief to the grim game of money-making. Tony's eyes are immediately centred on Linda. He sits beside her and openly flirts with her during every pause in the game.

Suddenly I'm overcome with despair. I get up from the table and go out on the veranda and cry. My dreams are crashing down. The poverty, isolation, and my son's illness have disheartened me and I've lost respect for the man I love. He can't offer protection to the baby and me. My stay in the Mercer has ruined my spontaneity. The world looks grim. Someone else is better able to care for my baby. I mull over my own actions since leaving the reformatory. They seem wanting.

As I take the train to New Brunswick, my mind turns toward other sights. I'm not returning with any sense of contrition, so my resentment towards my father remains, though of course it will never be spoken. My silence is taken for granted. My tongue has been bartered—I'm the child who may be seen but not heard. It's the bargain with my father for freedom from pregnancy.

—

*S*oon after my arrival in Saint John, my father and I go to the post office. It's now 1943. National Selective Service cards have been out for about a year. I had obtained mine in my married name, Yip. I'm aware of the stigma of a Chinese name for a white woman. My father and I advise the clerk that I have never had a card. The clerk issues one in my maiden name.

I haven't been in my father's home since I was sixteen and he put me on the train to Toronto. I'm now twenty-two. The house is luxurious compared to the places I've been during the past six years. I also have a permanent job in the theatre—it's easier than waitress work, which is strenuous. I've been getting overtired, quitting and starting over.

—

*M*y father sold his restaurant several years ago. Now there's a lineup of people waiting to get in; business is good for the new owners who are brothers. They're the in-laws of my father's former partner. When I tell my father that Nick, one of the brothers, tried to seduce me on my trip to Toronto when I was sixteen, he says angrily, "I wouldn't have sold him the Paradise if I'd known!" Nick had taken me to a rented hotel room while we were on a stopover in Montreal. When he started to take his clothes off I told him I had to go to the bathroom. Then I walked down the stairs and onto the street. Nick looked shaken when later he found me at the railway station.

Due to war regulations my father is required to go on salary. He cannot therefore reap profits from increased theatre ticket sales in the booming economy. He is trying to find some way to replace some of his lost income. He fills the theatre to capacity, breaking the rules of the fire department.

My brother is selling the hundreds of pipes located in the basement of his tobacco store that my father bought for him. He sits by an electric heater to keep his legs warm. A woman he employed sold some toothpaste over the price allowed by the wartime prices regulations. It was reported, and an officer came into his store and checked out the price of everything in it.

Sometimes I fearfully walk home in the blackout that's been imposed by the army to prevent enemy attacks, barely able to see the sides of the buildings or anyone on the street.

I hear secrets—German submarines are operating in the St. Lawrence.

It's the fourth year of the war, 1942, and Saint John is visited by many merchant seamen whose ships carry cargo across the Atlantic to England. The ships travel in convoys for protection from German submarines. Sometimes a ship takes a chance and goes it alone.

There's an urgent radio broadcast about some men who have stolen liquor from a ship. It's wood alcohol and they've gone blind!

—

I'm moving into a rooming house on Union Street. I'm glad to move out of my father's home where my presence is undermining efforts to preserve the Greek language. Accommodation is scarce in this booming wartime port. Eventually there will be fifteen French-Canadian girls and two English-speaking girls including me in the house. The French-Canadians come into Saint John from the country; some can't speak English. I assist in deciphering English documents. The girls share rooms in twos and four girls live in one large front room. They're getting jobs in factories and restaurants. Now there are other jobs than housework. There's a community kitchen in the house but only the factory girls use it since girls who work in restaurants are entitled to meals. One factory worker shows me the rash on her arms from the chemicals in the wood used for airplanes.

Coupons are issued to each person to limit consumption of butter, sugar, and alcohol. Nylons have just arrived and I buy mine on the black market. I help with the cash and checking the heavy winter coats at a dance hall on Saturday nights in West Saint John. It's called the French Hall and sometimes I get into a round of square dancing. It's always packed. It seems like French-Canadians never get tired of square dancing. A girl can be seen resting her head on her partner's shoulder, being passed from one man to another, as they spin around.

I notice that a few French girls have dark complexions, which may indicate they have Native blood. The French Canadians don't seem to care. Despite the crowded conditions, I'm able to bring Harry Junior to Saint John. I decide he will become a French Canadian.

I have no trouble retrieving young Harry from the Infants' Home when I arrive in Toronto. He is now four years old and still has eczema on his face. I tell my husband that I want to take our son to Saint John. He has little to say, since he cannot support a family. Neither have I expressed any interest in returning to extreme poverty. He knows I'm working for my father, that I have roots in Saint John, and he believes my father is rich. It's unlikely that his visits to see little Harry at Mrs. Stanley's are very rewarding (Mrs. Stanley looked after young children for the Infant's Home). When visiting his son in a white family's home, he must retain a certain formality—he must he polite and obsequious, and his child will not recognize him. He expresses no objections to my taking Harry to New Brunswick.

I don't tell my father that I'm bringing Harry to Saint John and, if he finds out, it will never be mentioned. Although my father and I live in the same city, we don't come into contact with each other except at the theatre. We don't frequent the same streets and our circles of friends are miles apart. The only people entering my father's house are Greek. My friends are all French Canadians.

I spend all my time with Harry except for five hours a day when I'm at work. There's always someone about to care for him in my absence and the girls are family-oriented, many coming from large families. However, the crowded conditions for Harry and me are too much. I place Harry with a middle-aged married French-Canadian couple I know well and take the train to Montreal. I'll arrange to board Harry in a convent and go to work. On arrival in Montreal I get accommodation at the YWCA. Due to overcrowding, the beds are about one foot apart. The following day I visit a convent and speak to a nun. She promises to see what she can do, telling me to come back in two weeks.

I'm not prepared for such a wait so my stay in Montreal requires that I must find work. I get a job as cashier in a delicatessen and sit in a cubicle similar to that in my father's theatre. Along with accepting payment for packaged food, I sell cigarettes from under my counter. One day, my employer says that six large packs of cigarettes are missing, the kind I don't smoke. I declare my innocence. When asked by the sweeper to remove myself to clean up, it had not occurred to me that I was risking a theft. Another theft was discovered—someone was putting boxes of food from the store out in the alley to be picked up. My employer says, "Someone could walk out with the scales and you wouldn't know."

When I return to the convent, the nun says, "I'm sorry but we couldn't find a placement for a sick child."

I had been gone for three weeks. What a terrible surprise! Harry's eczema had spread over his face and someone had reported him to the Children's Aid. I visit him in a large house but cannot take him out. I have to go to the Juvenile Court to retrieve him. I visit the court and take three French Canadians for character references, including the woman who was caring for Harry. I recognize the judge as the Anglican Church minister my mother visited in Quebec City when I was eleven years old. My mother had looked in the newspaper and found that the Anglican Church had been left a lot of money. My mother's family are Anglican so we went to the rectory to ask for assistance.

The judge interviews the witnesses. After they are gone he says, "Not one of them was clean—I wouldn't leave my child with any of them!"

The judge says he'll write to Mr. Yip to come and get Harry. I give him my husband's address. Harry has been with me for over a year and is now five years old.

My husband has come to Saint John by train, retrieved Harry, and taken him back to Toronto. He places our son in Mrs. MacTavish's preschool in the Chinese Canadian Institute on University Avenue where he is taught Chinese with both Chinese and several half-Chinese children. By the time I return to Toronto, Harry has been returned to the home of his foster mother, Mrs. Stanley. My husband tells me that, with his long hours of work and Harry's poor health, he couldn't manage.

CHAPTER 15

J am now living on Church Street with my mother and taking a secretarial course. On completion of my course I see nearby, on Church Street, the Chung Kee Laundry. The owner, Lew Yuen, allows me to take a room on the third floor of the old building. I paint the staircase as a prelude to my son's return. Lew hires painters to paint the kitchen. They spray-paint right over the cobwebs on the ceiling.

Harry is now seven years old. We sleep in a large double bed. The room is bare; there's no linoleum on the floor. We eat our evening meal with Lew and Chong, Lew's assistant, in the kitchen on the second floor. My son seems content to come under his mother's care. Lew is always in the laundry to supervise Harry after school. Harry attends Hester How school. It's not far from where my mother is now operating a tea room on Gerrard Street and Harry goes there for his noon meal. I arrive home from the office after five. But Harry's health is disabling. He suffers from severe asthma and the skin on his face needs constant attention to prevent it from becoming unsightly. On one occasion, when Harry's breathing was terribly laboured, I called the doctor. He said, "That child should never have been born." He agreed that a change of climate might help.

Harry tells me that some children waylaid him on the way home from school and threatened to beat him up. I tell him to take another route.

I'm working under my maiden name. No one at work must know I'm married to a Chinese. When my son and I go out, we remain on streets where encounters with my fellow employees are unlikely. At work, conversation is restricted. It's more relaxing to take my coffee break alone where I don't have to be on guard.

—

On some days the strong smell of bleach that whitens sheets and shirts emanates from behind the store where the tubs, washing machines, and drying racks are located. That's where Chong works. The smell goes upstairs to the second floor but tends to dissipate before reaching Harry's and my bedroom on the third floor. Chong's and Lew's rooms are also on the third floor. The collars of men's shirts have to be starched. Several heavy irons are heated on a stove and regularly exchanged. All bedding appears smooth and snowy white.

A large red sign with black letters erected on the storefront of the three-storey building says, "Chung Kee Laundry." The store is painted bright red. Customers climb the few steps to enter. From a window opening onto the entrance to the stairway, I see Lew constantly ironing. The opening also allows for the fresh air from the door as it is opened and closed. The coal stove on which the irons are heated and regularly exchanged is hidden from sight by the back of shelves.

Lew jokes with his customers as he retrieves one of the flat brown packages with Chinese characters from one of the shelves in full view of the counter. I overhear a customer complain but Lew remains cheerful. "You no like starch in the collar. If customer not satisfied I do over again. I don't mind."

I ask Lew why old Chong, his helper, always remains in the back of the store. Lew explains, "He no like to come in the front—he don't know English. If someone speaks to him he don't say anything like he don't hear."

Lew shows me a Christmas card he got from a woman in Australia. "She send me a card every Christmas," he says.

"How many years has she been sending it?" I ask.

"Long time," he says, "many years. She used to stay here; she remember the time she come into the laundry and ask me if she can stay. It was winter, very cold, lots of snow. I say, 'Sure I have room upstairs.' She stay here two years, then she go to Australia."

A girl, I think, cloistered in a Chinese laundry. How many Lew Yuens, I wonder, cared for destitute women in those hungry days?

I think of myself, how I don't go out at night, have no place to go. Like the Australian girl, I'm hidden away.

It was decided that Harry should go to Hong Kong and live with Lew's sister, Lu Bak-su. Lew assured me Harry would be fine. His health would improve and he would learn to speak Chinese. My husband signs papers approving his son's move out of the country.

I put Harry on the plane by himself, give him sufficient money, and tell him to be sure and put ointment on his face often. By the time he reached Hong Kong, Lew's sister would take over. It was one month before Harry's tenth birthday. I paid his fare from savings from my office work and Harry Senior's monthly payments for Harry. Besides, there was little expense because Lew Yuen didn't charge me for the room or for Harry's and my meals.

Then disaster struck. When Harry arrived at Kai-Tak International Airport in Hong Kong, Lu Bak-su wasn't there. There had been a misunderstanding concerning the date. A call was put over the radio to find Lu Bak-su. Reporters from the *China Mail* in Hong Kong converged on Harry and a reporter visits me at the laundry. Later he phones, asking me for a picture of my son. I refuse. Knowing that my employer is unaware of my Chinese connection, the reporter says, "You know I'm keeping your name out of the paper." I succumb but don't give him the picture he wants.

The contents of the interview are exaggerated, even false. The dire fate that awaits a child of interracial heritage is stressed. On September 2, 1949, the *Telegram* reads, "Double Colour Line Faced Harry Yip Here, Hong Kong Less Cruel." It goes on to say that "Because he was half white the Chinese youngsters in Toronto called Harry Yip 'Indian.' They teased him with 'Hiya, Siwash!' Because he was half Chinese the white children tormented him with 'Hello Chink!'"

One article concludes, "Harry, don't forget, is a Canadian despite his mixed-up parentage."

Harry's former foster mother is reported as being shocked. "Surely his mother couldn't have realized the conditions in China, or the state of Harry's health."

It seems that no reporter interviewed my husband or any member of the Chinese community. At any rate my husband would have refused to see him. Lew Yuen had wisely told me not to speak to the reporter who had come to the laundry looking for me. Another headline stated, "Toronto Boy Transplanted to Swarming Hong Kong." Harry was being removed from a comfortable Canadian home to a crowded place where black bugs could be found in the rice. In the meantime, although he was physically taken care of by Canadian Pacific airlines personnel, one reporter wrote, "He has the worst case of eczema I've ever seen."

I can't help wondering whether, if Harry's father had been Caucasian instead of his mother, this publicity would have been so intense. The publicity was a black eye for the already isolated Chinese community. A Chinese man phoned Lew and told him to kick me out.

I'm overwhelmed by the distortion of the reporter's remarks, especially the word "Siwash." I feel sure that the children at the Chinese school Harry attended after regular school hours would never say such a thing. I go to the newspaper office and ask to speak to the editor. I tell him the word "Siwash" was misrepresented. I used the word to emphasize the need for Harry, who resembles his father, to learn the Chinese language or be isolated. The editor appeared annoyed with his reporter but would not comply with my request.

My life is already one of alienation from society. I spend my evenings alone listening to the music of the big bands on the radio. It's a world from which I'm excluded. It seems I'm tainted by all Caucasians and I want nothing to do with them. Now I have distanced myself from the Chinese. I'm unaware that in the past it was the custom for Chinese to send their children to China for a few years. It's unlikely that the older Chinese would read the newspapers but I'm sure they would agree with my intention.

My chest feels heavy and my heart is breaking. I go to a Chinese medical doctor and request sleeping pills. When Lew and Chong go out on Sunday, I take ten or more, as many as I can. However, my stomach revolts, just as it did in the Mercer Reformatory when I took the experimental pills. I throw up on the floor in the hall. By this time my legs are weak. I get a rag but can barely clean up the mess.

I awake with my mother shaking me. "I'm sending you to the hospital!" she says.

"No, no, I don't want to go!" I cry out. Lew shields me with his arm to prevent my mother from carrying me off. My mother reconsiders. Suicide is a criminal offence; the penalty is two years. The following week, when not sleeping, I still move as if drunk.

My disgraced position demands that I leave Toronto. My brother had already committed suicide in Saint John two years before, a conclusion my mother refuses to believe. My father said it was due to health reasons. Now, my mother says, "I'll give you the money to go—it's yours from a property I sold."

I decide to join Harry in Hong Kong; he's been gone for four months. I go to a Citizenship and Immigration office in Toronto to obtain a

Canadian passport. An RCMP officer informs me that, because my husband is a Chinese National, I am a citizen of China by marriage.[1] He writes down "Chinese citizen." Then he takes me to a high desk for fingerprinting. He takes my hand and presses my little finger on a pad and moves it to another for imprinting, which he also does with every finger.

Obviously, a Canadian passport is beyond my reach. I'm disappointed. The officer gives me what I believe is an application for citizenship form to fill out. I understand that it takes five years to become a citizen. There's only one thing to do. I have to apply for a Chinese passport. Years later I will learn that the form I filled out was not an application for citizenship but a Declaration of Intention.

It's 1949 and the Canadian government recognizes the nationalist government of Chiang Kai-shek. They retain an embassy in Toronto. I find a mansion secluded behind a high hedge and go in. The Chinese man who interviews me is puzzled and non-committal at my request. I wait for several weeks but no passport is forthcoming. I now realize that a Chinese nationalist passport might not give me access to Hong Kong. The British government recognizes the Chinese Communist government. How can I contact them? My position seems hopeless.

There's only one way. I resign from my position with the department of immigration in Toronto and head for Vancouver. From Vancouver I make out an application for a Canadian passport in my maiden name. It warns there's a five-year term of imprisonment for false declaration, but I'm desperate so take the risk. My Canadian passport arrives. I write to the department of citizenship and immigration and cancel my earlier application.

CHAPTER 16

Jt's spring of 1950 when I board a Danish freighter of the East Asiatic Company bound for Singapore with stopovers in Japan and Hong Kong. A man in uniform assists me up the swinging gangplank. Another man follows behind carrying my suitcase and a case containing my typewriter. My suitcase is the size of a small trunk, brown leatherette over a light wooden frame, with two strong handles. My husband bought it for me some years ago for ten dollars.

The cabin assigned me is big enough for a least two people. I eat at the captain's table with several officers. My place is on the right-hand side of the captain. Breakfast is brought to my cabin. A light tap at the door wakens me and, when I answer, a tray is brought in and placed on the table. Two pleasant young stewards take turns bringing it in. From the steward I learn I'm the only passenger and the crew consists of forty-six men. Perhaps this is because of the Korean war.

Only the bare horizon can be seen. I'm free to roam but seldom go near the railing on the ship, which seems to be constantly tossing. I prefer to hang onto the guardrails on the ship's hull when moving about. I feel nauseated so do a lot of sleeping or just lying in my bunk with my eyes closed. I make sure I'm well rested for meal times.

Inside the cabin on the top deck is the ship's wheel and instrument panels. The radar is a separate piece of equipment and watching it is my chief occupation. It consists of a needle that goes around a circle like the second hand on a clock but it blurs when it encounters another ship or land.

The food is excellent but I never entirely relax in the dining room. I feel intimidated by the Danish officers with their uncreased uniforms, precise English, and cultured manners. The steward passes dishes from which to help ourselves. I don't know how to manoeuver the utensils so the steward, recognizing my difficulty, dishes out a portion of food onto my plate.

One day I arrive late for dinner. Everyone is standing, waiting for me. I sit down and then everyone else sits down. The captain scolds me for being tardy.

Early in the voyage an officer pursues me. When I don't return his affection he says, "Keep it!" and avoids me for the rest of the trip. Strangely, he says he's happily married in Denmark. The captain, a man verging on retirement, also speaks highly of his home in Copenhagen. I get the feeling that the Danes are a comfortably adjusted lot, satisfied to spend their days looking into the void that is the sea. However, I find looking at the flat horizon on all sides monotonous.

The ship suddenly jars. The captain says, "We hit something!" He tells an officer to steer the ship around the area, then dashes downstairs to the main deck and I follow. Two large patches of blood rise to the surface of the water. "We hit a mother whale feeding her young," says the captain. "If we had time I'd bring it aboard."

As we near Japan it becomes foggy. The captain tells me, "Something made of wood might not appear on the radar." He is apprehensive, stands for hours on the bow of the ship watching out for small boats.

It's sunrise and I spot a boat. Someone wearing a cone-shaped hat is moving the boat by pulling an oar back and forth. These fishing boats known as sampans become more numerous. Then Fujiyama appears—a large pyramid, a volcano. Even the sky looks different, the clouds being less dispersed than in Canada, perhaps due to less wind. Our ship anchors in the harbour from where I can see dozens of sampans clustered together on shore. Several Japanese, wearing white caps and gloves and rubber boots that separate the large toe, jump smartly aboard from a modern motorboat. They clamber toward the upper deck.

The next morning we leave. The captain says that in three or four days we will reach Hong Kong. The reality of being in a strange land frightens me—how to manage? Will I find work? By myself, I cry a little. When I speak of my fears to the crew, I'm assured there are automobiles and no grass huts in Hong Kong. "Where do you think you're going anyway?" one man asks. As far as anyone knows, I'm going for adventure. No one questions this as these seafarers are probably an adventurous lot.

We are now in the Orient and a certain stillness prevails. The sun shines benignly and the wind abates. Even the personality of the men seems to change—they've become quiet. There's a feeling of expectation. A huge unjagged mountain, Hong Kong, appears looming over an immense harbour with ocean liners and small craft. Ferries can be seen plying back and forth between Victoria Island (which is Hong Kong) and Kowloon. The ship is anchored across Victoria Inlet near Kowloon on the Chinese mainland. Like Hong Kong, Kowloon is also a British Protectorate. It has taken eighteen days to reach Hong Kong since boarding the freighter in Vancouver.

Within minutes a British official has boarded the ship and is stamping my passport. Immediately my luggage is passed to the operator of a boat about twelve feet long that has pulled alongside the freighter. I sit under a canvas roof with side flaps as the motor putt-putts slowly. As we move closer to Kowloon, I see the same cluster of sampans as in Japan. Entire families are living on boats, many of which are twelve to fourteen feet long. On one of these I see a large striped grey cat with a collar tied to the bow, sitting patiently. I remember what Lew Yuen had said, that cats from Canada had been shipped to China to catch rats. "Chinese cats are lazy!"

There's a lot of noise and activity on the dock. Barefoot Chinese coolies wearing torn shorts and sleeveless shirts are carrying heavy loads. Over one shoulder is a stick from which, at each end, a rope is suspended. At the end of each rope is a filled container of something or other. These labourers are bent over on one side from the weight of their loads as they walk or run. A taxi draws up and the driver seizes my luggage and assists me into the car. I say, "Take me to the Kowloon Hotel" which is where the Danish crew advised me to go.

There are no traffic lights and pedestrians dash out of the way as my taxi careens down the street. At the hotel, I book a room with two beds. Then I take a taxi to Lu Bak-su's address to find Harry. It's located in a poor district of Kowloon and a crowd gathers to see what a white woman is doing there. I climb two flights of stairs and there's Harry in an open area with other children. I walk over to him, put my arms around him, and cry. Harry takes a moment to fully recognize me. He says, "I thought your hair was darker." I'm surprised to see that for the first time since birth, Harry's eczema is entirely gone.

Poor Lu Bak-su. She had to contend with reporters during Harry's arrival and assure them she would provide him with butter and milk. Now I have come without prior notice to take him away. She wants to be sure that I am indeed Harry's mother. I pay for a taxi to take the three of us to the Canadian consulate. It's in Hong Kong, which means taking the ferry.

The Canadian consul asks me for my passport. I cringe. Harry's passport is in his Chinese name, "Yip." Mine is in my maiden name. The discrepancy will be obvious—I'll face arrest.

I say, "I left my passport at the hotel in Kowloon."

The official presents a letter I had sent him from Canada. It's signed in my married name, "Yip." He asks me to sign the name in order to compare the signatures and shows them to Lu Bak-su, which satisfies her that I'm Harry's mother.

After Lu Bak-su left, the Canadian official says, "I would advise you to take the first boat back to Canada. Hong Kong is not a place for a woman alone. A thief grabbed the arm of an English woman as she was walking on the street and ripped off her bracelet." I acknowledge his concern but fail to mention I have no fear of the Chinese and my physical safety is not the issue.

Harry visits some Chinese friends he knows, and I explore my surroundings. English soldiers are stationed in army barracks. They can usually be seen in twos walking the streets. I meet two of them and they invite me to their canteen. We have coffee and I'm surprised to see a can of Pacific condensed milk on the table. It's the first time I've seen anything but skim milk since arriving.

"There are 35,000 British soldiers in the colony; we know we could never hold back the Chinese if they decided to attack," one of them tells me.

The soldiers appear to be in their teens. They both have brown hair cut short, and are of slight or medium build. They're wearing khaki uniforms that appear to be too heavy for the warm weather. The conversation drifts into an exchange between the boys on the efficiency of their guns. I'm bored and get up to leave. It's an unexpected gesture and the young men look upset. Perhaps I vaguely remind them of home. I imagine they're homesick.

One of them says, "You won't talk to us after you've been here for awhile." I assure him I will but soon learn that the population hardly respects the British soldier—he has little money. This is in contrast to American sailors off warships who can be seen with all the pretty girls.

—

*M*y son and I find ourselves sharing a flat in Kowloon with Jennie Chen, an attractive twenty-four-year-old woman who speaks fluent English. Together we had the seven hundred American dollars to pay to the previous occupant. The rent is HK$1200 a month, which is $200 in American money. The apartment is located on a side street off Nathan Road about ten blocks from the ferry. It has a dining room, three bedrooms, an amah room, a small kitchen, and a toilet with basin. The floor is tile.

Jennie advises we must rent one of the bedrooms to reduce expenses. She knows a girl who makes her living by soliciting. She's quiet and won't bother us.

I place Harry in a Catholic school in Kowloon for HK$50 a month ($10 Canadian) and buy him a school uniform. I put my business college diploma into a frame and tack it onto the wall and get a couch to sleep and sit on and a table that seats six. Harry sleeps in the amah's room, which has two bunk beds.

What is common knowledge to Hong Kong natives has to be learned. The two-wheeled rickshaw is tilted back. It requires a certain trust. It's raining and under the black protective flaps I can't see anything. The shoeless runner is taking me somewhere. Without accurate directions a driver may take a person to the wrong place. On and on we go, never stopping until I realize that something is wrong. When I get out and pay the fare, I'm completely lost. As I try to make my way back I'm stepping over young men who are sleeping on bamboo mats. They pay no attention to me. Jennie tells me about an American sailor who was taken to the wrong address and refused to pay.

"He was hit on the head with a rock. It served him right!" she says.

A large cockroach flies into the window. Harry looks behind my dresser before going to bed. Jennie says, "Why are you afraid of them? They're only little creatures—we used to play with them when we were children."

Jobs are scarce. A Hong Kong newspaper states that one advertisement for an office clerk resulted in over 140 applications. Skilled businessmen expelled from China by the communists may have contributed to this overabundance of highly qualified personnel.

I put an advertisement in the newspaper to teach English and shorthand. It states only my address. Telephones are expensive.

Later I obtain a position teaching shorthand and typing at a Chinese school called the Institute of Business Administration, which is up the mountain in Hong Kong. The pay is low, and one meal is provided.

An American woman visits the school. I'm teaching American shorthand, Gregg. It's the same one she knows. She obviously needs work.

"We could put an advertisement in the paper asking for a secretary. When someone applies we could tell them they need more training and direct them to the school," she says. How cruel, I think, and exhibit no interest.

I'm exhausted from taking buses and ferries. When the deluge of rains come, I wade through ankle-deep torrents of water with my shoes; rubbers would be too hot. I'm becoming breathless from constantly talking and dictating. My income is barely enough to pay the expenses for Harry and me. I don't think of writing to my husband for money because I don't think he'll send it. He's angry because I left him. Later I think it was a mistake; he would have sent money for Harry.

I open my door and collapse. Helen and the amah pick me up. It's happened before—I awoke to find I had wet my bed; I tried to get up but my legs were paralyzed. I crawled towards the door and managed to open it. What's wrong? I visit a Chinese woman doctor.

"I must have malaria or some strange tropical disease," I say.

"I can't find anything wrong with you," she says.

Then I see in the newspaper where someone died from using a charcoal heater, which had used up all the oxygen. I had used a charcoal heater in my room for warmth when taking a bath in a metal tub.

Behind an enclosure off a Hong Kong street is a pawnbroker. I extend my arm and reach up to place my diamond ring into the hand of the lender. Later I retrieve my ring. This exchange happens often.

The cold season is upon us. A student gives me a baby-sized hot-water bottle to carry under my padded Chinese jacket.

This morning Helen shows me a tiny lizard she found in her bed. "They bite," she says.

We have a grouchy amah. She's a woman about fifty or so with a bun at the back of her head. I requested something of her only once, when a Chinese lady visited me and I asked her to bring tea. She did it ungraciously, rattling the dishes and setting the tray down with a bounce. My guest said that when she asked for me, the amah had said, "You mean the white devil who lives here?" But she's good with Harry. I didn't know he had a rash on his legs until I saw her washing them while Harry was standing in a tub of purple water. The Chinese medicine worked; Harry's legs got better.

Harry steals his school uniform out of the laundry where it's put to be washed. We can't afford a second one.

Jennie believes she treats our amah fairly. She tells me that the girls in the house next door make their amah get up late at night to serve them. Still, I heard Jennie speaking sharply to the amah.

Jennie doesn't say anything to me and I don't ask what happened but we have a new amah. She's young with braided hair down her back to indicate she's unmarried. She's wearing an outfit that looks like black pyjamas, as did the previous amah. Helen asks her to take me to a beauty parlour where I can get a cheap permanent. The amah will not be seen with me so she walks ahead and I follow. She takes me to a shop on a busy Kowloon street. The hairdressers are all men. She speaks to one of them and then leaves. The amah returns later and I follow her home. She tells Helen, "It's the first time I've seen a white devil with no money."

I teach Gregg shorthand—the dictation is mostly in English. I also teach English grammar. Three daughters of the Korean consul come for a lesson to my home. Their name is Lee and the girls range in age from fifteen to twenty-four years. They can't speak English so we use a dictionary to communicate. The girls come a few minutes early and wait in the dining room.

Then what should happen but our roommate walks in with two sailors in white uniforms, middies, and bellbottom trousers! It's a catastrophe! The girls will tell their parents who would not want their daughters exposed to sailors. They will discontinue their lessons, which would be a terrible loss—I'm being reasonably well-paid for the girls.

When the lesson is over I accost Jennie. "Our roommate will have to get out!"

Jennie tries to placate me. "It won't happen again," she says.

The next day the Korean vice consul visits me. He advises that, in the future, the girls will attend the school where I'm teaching after class.

Our roommate is a furtive person; she doesn't take any meals with Jennie, Harry, and me. I surmise she speaks a little English. She's thin, of average looks, and probably bordering on thirty. Jennie and I discuss what will become of her. "She can always find an English soldier," Jennie says.

Jennie is attending classes in flower arrangement and is always trying to improve her English. Her British boyfriend stays with her one or two nights when his ship is in port. Jennie tells me that he's studying for his captain's papers. She says, "The only reason people come here is because they can't get along at home. I think if you're nice everyone will like you."

I resent her remark; it will be easier for her than for me. When she marries, her Caucasian husband will be respected and provide protection.

Jennie is aware of my financial difficulties but doesn't suggest a solution. She mentions girls working in a dance hall being paid for dances. I would make more money but I don't want to shock my students. But aside from that is the fear. The Canadian consul might not approve of a Canadian woman working in a dance hall. The risk of their discovering my false passport is frightening.

Harry will be twelve years old next month. He has been in Hong Kong for two years and speaks Chinese well enough and his health has improved. But I've been coughing a lot and my left lung feels sore—what would happen if I got sick? A British police officer I know said I could be deported back to Canada as an indigent. How terrible! I'm sending Harry back to his father in Canada. I know he cares about Harry. At one time, he had said, "I don't want to lose my wife and child." Harry Senior answers my telegram, "I'll be waiting."

Jennie pays me back the key money I'd invested in our apartment and I put Harry on the airplane for his return trip to Canada to his father.

*C*HAPTER 17

J'm returning to Canada. Christmas of 1951 has passed and Mr. Fong, principal of the school, has written a recommendation. I've borrowed money from a friend in Canada to pay for my return voyage. Now, after all the rewards I've experienced, I can't bear to leave. From being an outcast I became an esteemed member of society in this new land. Here, although peopled primarily by Chinese, there are Eurasians, Philippinos, Portuguese, and Indians. It's said that Caucasians make up only five percent of the population. The colony is administered by the British who have government offices, maintain an army, and hold major positions in the police force, and of course there are the airline pilots and stewardesses who patronize the hotels and European YMCA. There are British shipping companies and import-export businesses.

I know I can't stay but in one last spin of the wheel I imagine that, if I could only find some way of making enough money, my husband would send Harry back. I apply for a secretarial position with an import-export firm. An affable middle-aged British gentleman invites me into his office for an interview and I sit on a brown upholstered leather chair. He says, "Well, tell me, what brings you to Hong Kong?" He smiles amiably and leans back in his chair.

"I consider that to be entirely my own business," I say, and get up to leave.

My prospective employer is astonished—he sputters with embarrassment. "Well—I, I didn't mean to pry!"

I know I'm completely rude but my hoping for a miracle has undermined my social graces.

It's January 1952 when I board the *China Mail*, an American freighter, for my return trip to Canada. As it pulls out I gaze at the ships in the beautiful harbour, the ferry winding its way back and forth between

Kowloon and Hong Kong, the large luxury liner at the dock in Kowloon, and the smaller ships moving about in the shimmering water. This new world has given me a freedom from fear of rejection and a respect I've never known. But my reveries are not without regret: I never kept my promise to myself that Harry and I wouldn't return to Canada for five years.

Among the returning passengers is a missionary family expelled from China by the communists. Although I'm sitting across from them in the dining room, they're not friendly. I think it's because I play cards with the crew at night or they may be distraught. My best friend Jane, a Chinese girl from the school, took me to meet a grey-haired missionary woman who cried openly—she was returning to England after a lifetime in China. She had lost touch with everyone she had known in England. I felt sorry for her but Jane, who comes from Szechuan province, was not sympathetic. She said, "The missionaries used to have parties and eat cakes and the Chinese weren't invited."

One man in the import-export business said he offered to work for the communists but wasn't permitted to stay.

In just over two weeks the ship arrives at the Vancouver dock and two uniformed men come into my cabin, pushing their way around. They spy the can of cheese I'm bringing to Canada for a friend and take it away. One of the men asks me where I'll be staying.

"At the Hazelwood Hotel," I say. It's operated by a Chinese man and his Caucasian wife on Hastings Street, a seedy street in Vancouver where rooms are cheap. It was where I lived while awaiting my passport to leave Canada for Hong Kong two years before. Within a couple of days, the cheese is returned.

I send a telegram to Lew Yuen requesting money for my fare to Toronto. There's no reply. I cannot tarry long as I'm running out of money. I answer an advertisement for a secretarial position with the Powell River Company (which turns out to be a paper mill). The next day I take the ferry to Powell River up the British Columbia coast and am lodged in a company house. Having a permanent address, I write to Harry at my husband's address.

The reply is shocking. Harry's letter states that he wants to stay with Mrs. Stanley, his former foster mother. The letter is from her address on Prescott Avenue. I thought he was living with his father. I panic. Harry hadn't seen or mentioned her since he was seven years old. He's now twelve. Did my husband take Harry to visit Mrs. Stanley when he returned to Toronto? I don't know, but I can imagine the scenario, the reliving of the shock of Harry's transfer to Hong Kong by Mrs. Stanley, her neighbours, and social workers who attend to the babies in her care. She must be reinforced by the newspaper article that insists, "Harry, don't forget, is a Canadian despite his mixed-up heritage." Harry will want to hide his mixed race.

Is that what happened to make Harry forget me so soon? Was Harry compelled to make a choice? We've been apart for less than six months.

"Could I please stay with Mrs. Stanley?" he writes. "I want to have a stable home."

Stable! Where did he get that word? There's no mention of his father.

My God! My husband has turned over my letter to our son. He knows that he's staying with Mrs. Stanley. He's condoning it! Did Harry never go to my husband when I sent him back? He's been living with Mrs. Stanley all this time? He's losing the Chinese language he's learned. I was depending on my husband to integrate our son into a culture that would give him some protection. Otherwise he'll suffer ostracism and there's nothing I can do. I think of the newspaper story about Harry's transfer to Hong Kong before I left Toronto. Mrs. Stanley told the reporter how shocked she was, how his mother couldn't have known what she was doing, that I had not acted in his best interest. How can I restore his faith in his mother? I have no support. I no longer have any Chinese friends. My husband has let me down and I have no resources. How can I ever return to Toronto and face the disgrace I experienced through the case's publicity? Neither can I face the humiliation that my son prefers another mother. I don't have a permanent home like Mrs. Stanley. I reconcile myself that his status with his foster mother may be more satisfying than sharing the fate of an excommunicated mother. A mother's isolation is passed onto her child. Does Harry sense this?

It doesn't occur to me that Harry is asking for my permission to stay with Mrs. Stanley, that he hadn't actually moved in with her.

I'm torn—Mrs. Stanley saved Harry's life when he was a baby. He wasn't walking when he was two—but then, I didn't know when babies start to walk.

I write back. "I won't stand in your way if you want to stay with Mrs. Stanley." Sometime later a social worker visits me in Powell River but she doesn't mention my husband. It's as if he doesn't exist. She also fails to mention that there's been a Family Court hearing—Children's Aid workers were noted for not revealing information. I'm vague about what to do about my son.

—

*T*he Powell River Company is a townsite and everyone in it works for the company. I share a company house with three other employees—two nurses and a young woman who works in the only retail store in town. Meals are served in the dining room of a house set aside for that purpose. I sit with the doctor, dentist, engineers, bank employees, and young women who are clerical workers. My job is secretary to the town-site manager.

Since leaving Toronto I have discarded my lifelong name (Velma) and call myself Mary. Now, because I get so much mail from my students and friends in Hong Kong, I'm dubbed "Hong Kong Mary."

I soon find there's a class divide. We don't associate with the mill workers although one nurse goes around with a mill manager. The other nurse is elderly and taciturn, and apparently plays bridge every evening. The two clerical workers go off in cars in a foursome with the two male bank employees. There's a shortage of women in this company town and an admirer has taken to sitting near me at the dinner table. One attractive woman with two children had declared herself a widow, come to Powell River to work, and within a short time married a mill supervisor.

However, a company town can be restrictive. No one in the dining room talks politics or religion or about their job. I'm not acquainted with small-town gossip and become fearful of the personal chitchat, possibly because I have so much to hide. As Maggie, the homegrown cook, says, "People come up from Vancouver and we don't know anything about them."

When I remark to another secretary that Powell River is beautiful with its huge dark trees, she says, "It only gives me claustrophobia."

One of the worst drawbacks of this picturesque town is the stench of sulphur coming from the mill; it's a smell that occurs often. Still, there are weekends when some of us women are driven in a small motor-boat up the Powell River to a simple summer resort. The narrow river is surrounded by mountains, and the water is warm and inviting, but I refuse to go skinny dipping at night—someone might see my breasts and suspect I've been a mother.

Another secretary has arrived from Vancouver. Rose is a tall, slightly overweight woman in her forties, unpretentious, with an open smile and large earrings. Whether or not she is respectable becomes a topic of interest and Rose is subjected to severe criticism. From being outgoing, she becomes reserved. We become friends and she confides her desire to meet a man with children and get married. I suggest an advertisement in the paper. Rose gets forty-seven answers. Of these she chooses one and agrees to meet him in Vancouver. When she returns she says, "He took me to a cheap restaurant and bought me a sandwich, then he said, 'I sure like a good fuck!'"

The secretive letters were to become Rose's greatest paranoia. She lost her purse containing several letters and she's sure someone has found it and read the letters. "I can't face them—they'll say I couldn't get a man, that I had to advertise for one."

So great was her shame that Rose didn't go to work but stayed in bed for three days. It began to affect me—after all I had suggested she advertise. Everyone was asking, "What was in the purse?" However, at the company party Rose re-established herself as a woman who can get a man. Bill, a highly valued engineer with the company, took Rose home from the party. The following day Rose tells me, "He drove the car to a quiet place and said, 'You're a woman of the world.'"

Rose laughingly describes the engineer's unseemly actions. "He was like a wild animal going after me—his nails tore into me."

Rose does not reveal how she resisted this sexual assault. Further, she fails to keep it a secret, especially from Gloria who works in the retail store. It's well-known that Gloria is in love, resigned to casting glances beneath her blonde lashes at Bill in the dining room. Gloria's disappointment becomes obvious. No longer does she attempt to sit at Bill's table. Her faith in the engineer and the fact he has chosen someone else has shattered her dreams.

—

I've been in Powell River for nine months but now I'm leaving. My secret life is less threatening in the big city. Once in Vancouver, I join the peace movement. In a frenzy of activity I'm directing my energies towards ending the Vietnam war. All racial prejudice appears to be suspended, at least for the time being; concern for personal matters has become irrelevant. After work every day, there are educational sessions, discussions, and strategies. On weekends there are socials—making sandwiches and serving drinks to raise money, or I stand on the street with a peace petition.

I meet Rose on the street in Vancouver. She magnanimously tells me with a big smile, "Someone phoned from the Children's Aid looking for you. No one could believe it—everyone was shocked—you married a Chinese!"

She keeps smiling and laughing at my deviance and how surprised she was. She invites me to visit her and dangling from the ceiling in her apartment are Chinese chimes.

———

*I*n 1962 Harry visits me in British Columbia. He's twenty-three. Neither of us mentions Hong Kong or the past.

I ask, "How's Mrs. Stanley?"

"She's fine" he replies.

I can't ask why he didn't go to his father when I sent him back to Canada from Hong Kong. There must be no opening of old wounds.

I ask, "Do you still have asthma?"

"I have it under control," he says almost inaudibly. I imagine it's a sore spot for him. His childhood health problems may be embarrassing. He has been working at the same office for a number of years.

"Do you have a girlfriend?" I ask. He vaguely suggests he has.

"What nationality is she?"

He refuses to answer. I name several nationalities but he is not deterred. I feel a certain resentment from him.

"It's hard being the only half Chinese around," he says bitterly.

"There are lots of Eurasians in Hong Kong."

"Yes, in Hong Kong," he says angrily, "but not here!"

It's my fault he was born—I feel the sting.

Harry becomes conciliatory. "Sometimes I'm taken for Italian," he says with satisfaction.

"If someone directs a racial remark to you, what do you say?"

"I tell them they're entitled to their own opinion."

"No! no! they're not!"

"Some people go up and others go down," he says as he walks away. I feel the words are directed at me but don't answer. It doesn't occur to me that he might know I was in the Mercer Reformatory. Did one of Mrs. Stanley's social worker friends tell her? Does Harry know? Mrs. Stanley used to tell me that when I came to take Harry out, he would hide. What would cause that?

My main objective is to impress Harry with my respectability. I need to dispel any negative impressions he may have regarding white women who marry out of their race. He will see me through the eyes of his friends who, based on his remarks, I'm convinced are all white. I'm now married to a white man and have two children; we own a house.

Now Harry is a stranger. There can be no explanations, no mention of the past. Wrong impressions may have congealed. I haven't left my mark on Harry. Or rather, not the mark I had hoped for.

Harry is also creating the impression of success. His shoes are shined and he's dressed impeccably. But beneath the surface of well-being is his awareness of the humiliation of his father and the omission of evidence at the Toronto Family Court hearing when he was twelve years old. He's not prepared to tell me what happened.

---

*L*ater I learn that Harry had gone to live with Mrs. Stanley in March of 1952, when I had been in Canada for about two months. There was a court hearing "to locate the mother." At the trial neither Harry Senior nor Dock Yip, my husband's lawyer, knew I was in the country, neither did Judge Mott, who presided over the hearing.

Mrs. Stanley and Harry remained silent in a conspiracy to conceal his mother's whereabouts and assure his placement with Mrs. Stanley.

In such a short time, six months—a long time for a child—Harry became convinced he had been ill-treated by his mother and father. Mrs. Stanley and her neighbours agreed that Harry was a Canadian boy. She would have shown Harry the article in the newspaper, a condemnation of his mother and father for sending him to Hong Kong.

In Mrs. Stanley's mind it would only be his mother who would stand in the way of Harry becoming a ward of the Children's Aid. Harry must have retrieved the letter I sent to him at his father's address without his father knowing. (I'd sent a letter to Harry at his father's address but Harry wasn't living with his father—he was living with my husband's friend Kwong. It's possible that Mrs. Stanley had Harry's mail transferred to her address.) He took it to Mrs. Stanley who dictated the letter to me—that he wanted a "stable" home. After I gave him permission, he must have left his residence where he lived under his father's care and moved in with Mrs. Stanley. It never occurred to me that my husband would be in Toronto Family Court. I thought he had abandoned Harry.

A social worker knew I was corresponding with Harry at Mrs. Stanley's address but the court was never informed. Records indicate that Harry could speak Chinese but this wasn't presented. My husband wasn't mentioned in Harry's letter nor by the social worker who interviewed me. Harry's father was irrelevant. No Children's Aid worker had contacted him regarding Harry's care prior to his leaving home. Tacit approval was given to his actions. Harry Senior didn't know where Harry went when he didn't return home. Neither was the court concerned with the breach of rules by the Children's Aid Society workers. It was only I who would be recognized as a complement to the proceedings of the court, despite my stigmatized marriage.

Harry Senior was required to answer questions—where I was born and about my religion, though neither of us went to church. He had to acknowledge knowing that my official name was Athena Mary though he knew me only as Velma.

Mrs. Stanley was asked to identify Mr. Yip to ascertain he was Harry's father. No marriage certificate was presented. She said she always called me by my maiden name, which she spelled incorrectly as "Miss Dennison," when in fact she always called me "Mrs. Yip." It was incorrectly stated that Harry had lived with Mrs. Stanley for most of his life.

Harry learned during court proceedings that his parents had not been married when he was born—it was a denigration of my character and a legal disadvantage before the court. I found out years later how the trial for Harry's wardship proceeded:

SOCIAL WORKER: This birth certificate was in the maiden name of the mother. She later married Mr. Yip and I think there must be a corrected verification of birth. Mr. Yip, do you know the date on which the child was born?

I forget it.

JUDGE MOTT: There it is, he doesn't know. What is your name?

Jim Yip (name changed from Harry to Jim)

Where were you born?

China.

And what is your religion?

United Church.

Where do you live, Mr. Yip?

385 Church Street.

Are you working?

No, I am not working for three months.

Are you the father of Harry Yip?

Yes.

And what was the name of Harry's mother?

Mary Athena, something like that.

My information is Velma Mary Athena Demerson. Are you married to her?

Yes.

Where was she born?

New Brunswick, Saint John.

What is her religion?

I don't remember what church.

Was she Protestant or Roman Catholic?

Protestant.

And where is she at the present time?

I don't know, I haven't any idea.

Do you know if she is in Canada?

No. She is in Hong Kong, the last time.

Where is Harry? Who is looking after Harry?

I was looking after Harry before.

Where is Harry now?

I don't know.

Do you think he may be in the care of the Children's Aid and Infants' Home?

I don't know.

Where was he living when you last knew where he was?

With a friend of mine.

What is the friend's name?

The friend's name is Kwong.

How old is he?

Twenty-five.

Mrs. Stanley, Do you know whether this man is the father of Harry Yip or not?

Yes, sir.

How do you know?

Because he used to visit the child.

And he came as the father of the child?

Yes, sir.

Mr. Yip, has this boy lived with you for any length of time?

I think about eight months.

That is all the time you have ever had him with you?

Yes.

Harry was examined by a doctor and found to be slightly under-nourished and small for his age. His teacher stated that he was coming to school sleepy. Harry said he wasn't getting proper food, that he was making his meals himself and eating tinned food.

When questioned by the judge, Harry said, "I would like to stay in one place. Usually when my mother or father take me we move away."

Harry became a ward of the Children's Aid. He was twelve years old.

***

J received a letter from Harry in 1964. He said that Mrs. Stanley had returned to England with her son. Later he wrote asking if I knew where he could find his father. I wrote back that I didn't know. Why would he be looking for his father when he abandoned him when I sent him back to Canada? It will be some time before I learn that it was not his father who had deserted him—it was Harry who had denied his father.

***

*H*arry drowned in 1966 while learning to swim. He was twenty-six years old. A letter from me was found in his pocket so I'm notified and attend the funeral. I learn that Harry had erased all reference to his mother and father and presented himself as a foundling raised by Mrs. Stanley. No one knew that his mother was white. The young man who was with Harry at Musselman's Lake where he died said, "Harry spoke to me that day about things he never talked about before."

At the funeral, the minister says, "If Harry had been born in the sixteenth century, he would be looked on as a saint."

"No, no," I say. "I don't want him to be a saint!"

CHAPTER 18

*I*t's a long way to Toronto by train from the province of my newly created life but I need time to plan. I've done everything I will ever do. I'm stepping out of my emotional attachments—an example of independence, for what it's worth. I am re-entering the place where part of me has always been, I'm going home to attend to "unfinished business." This is a term used in films where released penitentiary inmates are bent on settling "old scores"—but I'm going into a prison, not coming out. It's a lonely trail. I feel as if I'm entering a monastery, not a place of peace but of purgatory. I must relinquish all ties to the present and entomb myself in the past to affirm that it actually existed. There must be some crumbs to scavenge. There's been no revolution, no conflagration whereby everything was destroyed. It is my intention to transcend a formidable gap between the past and the present.

It's now 1989. It's a long way back—fifty years. Dr. Guest was in her fifties as I remember her. Or perhaps I'm mistaken. Young people sometimes see adults older. Perhaps she was in her forties. So she *might* still be alive—in her nineties. I'll look up her name in the telephone book, find her address, and go to her home, watch at the door, follow her. Perhaps I'll ring the doorbell. Someone will answer the door, her caregiver, herself. What will I say? I'll decide later. I'll find the church she goes to. I'll sit behind her and listen for every word, become friendly, gain access to her home, become her homemaker. I know how to ingratiate myself, applaud the industrious, decry the indolent, praise the successful, and condemn the poor. I know she feels no remorse. I need to be close, get inside her—wrest the power that she holds over me. Somehow, by some word of her, some glimpse of her personality, I'll find the answer—why, why?

I'm still afraid of her, physically. The doctor is a symbol of authority that shadows me. Why did she mutilate me, so brutally, so many times? Was she a sadist? Conducting an experiment? Was I a serious case for which no other treatment would suffice? Or was she committed to "hygienic" principles of racial superiority?

I arrive in Toronto and find her name in the phone book. There's someone with the same initials. I make the call. A voice tells me "there's no one here by that name." My efforts to locate her are fruitless. I search the obituaries. Dr. Guest died in 1958. I will have to start from scratch. I comb through the archives, looking for traces of my story.[1] What a shock! My mother had written to Dr. Guest the same day I escaped from the Toronto General, telling her to go ahead with the operation before I left the hospital! In the letter, my mother claims that she had written my father asking for the money for it. "He assures me he will pay the bill if it's necessary." She even suggests my approval of Dr. Guest. "She speaks well of your skills."

I can't believe it! My mother has practised this deception and kept it from me all these years. What kind of an operation is she talking about? Why the secrecy? I'm perplexed; there was nothing wrong with me to warrant an operation. Would she have given her permission, signed a document, and subjected me to sterilization without my knowledge? In hospital after giving birth, I would be none the wiser. I would be told there was a birth complication or that I needed an appendectomy.

Did the doctor tell my mother that I had a filthy disease, that she was doing her best, that only an operation would cure me? Had my mother held off until my escape caused her to act? She had dutifully visited me in the reformatory and endured my constant pleas for help. She had finally decided to stop the painful treatments. An operation would end the pain. Is that it? It was when I escaped that she wrote the letter.

My mother said in her letter, "Velma must not get on the table again without an anaesthetic." She had confronted the medical bureaucracy as best she could. Perhaps the removal of tissues by constant surgery could mean only one thing to her: cancer. My mother had only the experience of her past to rely on. My aunt Eva (my mother's sister), at twenty-four years of age, had been operated on and died of cancer. My mother must have thought I had cancer. What else could she have thought? She had only her family's definition of disease.

Dr. Guest's report states, "Mother's letter to be answered later after pelvic exam."

—

$\mathcal{T}$he Toronto General Hospital was informed on the day of my arrival that I was a Mercer Reformatory inmate. I find a report that includes my dates of arrest and entry into the industrial refuge, the charge of "incorrigible and unmanageable," the term of sentence, and my mother's address. Thus, hospital staff were aware during my stay that I was a prisoner.

Miss Milne's position as superintendent compelled her to report the escape of an inmate to Provincial Secretary Neelands. She advises, "About 1:15 AM yesterday (Sunday) a call from the Hospital stated that this patient had left the Hospital that morning between 1 and 2 AM, and that the police department had already been notified. However, the girl's mother telephoned the Hospital to say that the girl had gone home and she would bring her back at once so, within an hour after her departure from the Hospital, clad only in hospital bedclothes and slippers, she was again in care of the Hospital. I sent a matron and the babe for her at 8 AM the same day." It was October 30. I had been in the hospital for twelve days.

Miss Milne adds, "it was necessary from the time of her admission here to give her intensive and quite painful treatment for a social disease. In talking with her on her return yesterday, I found that it was fear of this medical treatment being continued that had made her run away. I was able to reassure her that there would not be any immediate treatment, and today Dr. Edna Guest reported that no further treatment of the rather severe kind would be required, in the meantime at any rate."[2]

The superintendent's letter must have had some effect because the next time I saw Dr. Guest she said, "This is the girl I have to use a lot of pain killer on." The drug was Novocaine.

Dr. Guest had been physician at the reformatory for nearly twenty years. She had close connections with the medical, military, and governmental personnel in the prison system. In 1922 when she first became a physician at the Mercer, gonorrhea statistics for the women there rose to 47 percent from 26 percent the previous year.[3]

—

$\mathcal{M}$y self-deprecation equals that of my mother. "I'm sorry for what happened," she said, even with her dying breath. She who had stood up against the world: the bureaucracies that she dreaded, the medical authorities, and the law. My mother always said she was a fast thinker. And her stories always involved her outwitting her captors—the insurance company when we had the fire, the welfare authorities harassing our tenants, the church that condemns divorce. My grandfather had once told her, "Never get tangled up with the law." My escape became hers.

But my mother had capitulated—she couldn't have told the judge she would take me home. "I shouldn't have listened to your brother," she said. Was it the love for my brother that overpowered her? She was compelled by sympathy and guilt to atone for his disability. I remember her crying in the middle of one night and then the next day she called the doctor. What she thought was rheumatism was infantile paralysis—polio. Her boyfriend had been carrying my brother to the bathroom. My mother used to say, "I don't believe in doctors."

My mother, so independent during her lifetime, had confronted a situation she could not imagine. Her own isolation through her daughter was emphasized by everyone around her, especially by my father, my brother, and probably by her boyfriend. For the first time in her life she didn't know what to do.

Now my inability to protect Harry against the psychological effects of a hostile world haunts me. Am I entirely at fault? My mother said, "I'm sorry." Now, just as my mother reflected on her own weakness at death, I'm destined to do the same. Guilt propels me forward.

I find my name on the Mercer Reformatory register and discover I was sentenced under the *Female Refuges Act*. I didn't know I was sentenced under an act. Just as I didn't understand when the judge said my offence was "Incorrigible." I finger my way through the *Canada Criminal Code*. The offence isn't there! There must have been a mistake. I should never have been imprisoned. It's only after the Ontario Archives locate a serological report with my name on it that I realize I had been used in a drug study. If I had known of the dangerous effects of these drugs, I wouldn't have taken them.[4] Harry would have been well and my marriage may not have broken up. Neither should the other girls have been imprisoned. Sue wouldn't have lost her children.

⁓

*I*n the University of Toronto medical library, I find a dusty box full of papers published in the 1920s. The papers describe "Social Health to Advocate the Knowledge and Practice of Social Hygiene as the One Way to Racial Improvement." They're published by a branch of the Canadian Social Hygiene Council; their slogan proclaims: "The Race is to the Strong." On one paper there's a picture of a family, and a caption beneath that says "The Fit and the Unfit to Carry on the Race." At one point the Social Hygiene Council changes its name to the Health League of Canada. "Dr. Edna Guest, Mercer Physician" is vice-president.

Dr. Guest believed in scientific heredity theories concerning the "feeble-minded" and "moral defectives," believed that only those versed in the mysteries of science could deal with the genetically diseased. From the point of view of the eugenicists, most of the women in the Mercer Reformatory were incurable moral degenerates due to inbred character defects. But to prove the physical basis of mental deficiencies, physical anomalies were required. In an article titled, "Glands Link with Crime," Dr. Guest claims that "many unsocial acts among women were due to the abnormal functioning of glands associated with the sex instinct." She suggests that studies should be done on Mercer women. Moral defectives could thus be linked, not only by observation, but by physical abnormality. The distinction between borderline or "high grade morons" and normal women could be confirmed. Normal women would no longer have to identify with the loose and immoral women who had demeaned their sex. Respectable women would no longer have to bear the disrespect and lack of equality with men. Dr. Guest would have had to examine over three hundred Mercer women the year the Belmont girls arrived. It's likely she spent more time on Helga and me than on the others. I underwent weekly treatments for over two months in surgery, injections, and chemical applications.

———

On October 10, 1939, a week before my baby was born, the provincial department of health sponsored a conference on venereal disease. World War II had begun exactly one month prior and the conference was called to determine ways to protect and treat the military. A number of research papers on the efficiency of drugs for venereal disease and the use of malaria and fever were presented. Dr. A.L. McKay, who had formerly visited the Mercer to treat inmates with syphilis, presented a paper entitled "Suggested Measures for the Control of Venereal Disease in the Civilian Population in Areas in which Troops are Mobilized." In regard to women charged with sex offences, he states, "This has been discussed with the Crown...and a scheme worked out whereby once these individuals are in custody they will be held for forty-eight hours without bail for examination for venereal disease."

"Dr. Edna Guest, director of the Veneral Disease Clinic, Women's College Hospital, suggested that Dr. Bates, through the Health League of Canada, approach the government with the view to putting recreational centres right in the barracks. Dr. Guest feels that some of the trouble could be eliminated if the soldiers had adequate and attractive recreational activities. Dr. Guest professed a willingness, both personal and through her clinic, to do anything that would in any way be of assistance." A couple of months later, on December 11, a "serious incident" occurred with a Mercer patient. On December 15, Dr. Edna Guest was no longer employed by the Department of Prisons and Reformatories.

My situation seems hopeless. How can I overcome the stigma imposed on me so many years ago? This image of me as deserving to be confined will be passed down to future generations of my family. On one occasion I screamed at my father, "You shouldn't have had me arrested."

My father retorted, "If I hadn't put you in there, you would have turned rotten."

Many of the mothers and grandmothers of our present generation have buried this episode of their lives, lest it tarnish their reputation. Whether guilty of wrongdoing or not, a woman having undergone the experience of imprisonment invites suspicion.

Sometime after my father died, I decided to visit some relatives on his side of the family. At one point I found myself protesting my father's role in my imprisonment. A female relative told me, "Your father didn't know that was going to happen. He only wanted to scare you." Then she lashed out in defence of him, and said, "I know all about you."

AFTERWORD

I was awarded the J.S. Woodsworth Prize for anti-racism by the New Democratic Party in March 2002.

In December of 2002 I received an apology from the Province of Ontario. Written by Attorney General David Young, the Minister Responsible for Native Affairs, the letter said:

> I am writing to you on behalf of the Government to apologize to you for your incarceration under the *Female Refuges Act* in the 1930s. This Act had unfortunate and unjustified consequences for you and other women who were unjustifiably incarcerated under its provisions.
>
> In addition, the government wishes to apologize for the adverse effects your incarceration undoubtedly had on your son, who was born to you while you were in custody, and to his father, Harry Yip.

This apology, given to my family, fails to mention *all* women incarcerated under the *Female Refuges Act*. Nevertheless, the implication is clear. It removes from women the stigma of wrongdoing in the eyes of the law and the public. The hundreds or thousands of women who were unjustly imprisoned between 1913 and 1964 are finally exonerated. The *Female Refuges Act* was linked to the eugenics movement and its pseudo-scientific belief that feeblemindedness and immorality were hereditary. Thus, it covered only women of childbearing age, fifteen to thirty-five. I feel fortunate to have been a survivor.

NOTES

CHAPTER 2

1 This rule was in place for a long time. According to the 1916 Rules Governing Inmates of the Mercer Reformatory for Ontario, "You are not permitted to sit on your bed, nor to lie on it, except when you undress and retire for the night. You must not remove your chair from its proper place nor move any of the furniture in your dormitory" (*Canada Gazette* July 28, 1917).

2 From the factory, women's clothing, pillow slips, sheets, towels, pillow cases, and other articles are sold to other institutions under the jurisdiction of the Province of Ontario (*Report of Prisons and Reformatories for 1933*, Mercer Reformatory, Department of the Provincial Secretary, Ontario Sessional Papers).

3 The act said: "The inspector may direct the removal of any inmate who proves unmanageable or incorrigible from an industrial refuge to a common gaol or to the Andrew Mercer Reformatory for Females" (*Statutory Orders and Regulations* 1937, c. 384). By the *Statute of Law Amendment Act*, 1939, section 12, the words "unmanageable or incorrigible" were removed.

4 "Girls Cry When Leaving Refuge for Reformatory. W.J. Jannett of the provincial secretary's department explained that the move had been made because there were so few girls at Belmont home on committal of magistrates" (*Toronto Star* July 19, 1939).

5 "The industrial refuge is in no way a prison, and...the life and the work here is in no sense a punishment. This is just what its name implies—it is a Refuge— a place of safety" (*1918 Annual Report* of the Toronto Industrial Refuge, the Aged Women's Home, and the Aged Men's Home).

6 "Everyone is a loose, idle or disorderly person or vagrant who (i) being a common prostitute or night walker, wanders in the fields, public streets or highways, lanes or places of public meeting or gathering of people, and does not give a satisfactory account of herself" (*Criminal Code of Canada*, RSC 1927, c. 36, s. 238[i]).

CHAPTER 5

1 "Everyone, above the age of twenty-one years, is guilty of an indictable offence and liable to two years imprisonment who, under promise of marriage, seduces and has illicit connection with any unmarried female of previously chaste character and under twenty-one years of age" (*Criminal Code of Canada*, *Offences Against Morality*, 1927, c. 36, s. 212).

2 Section 15 states that any female between the ages of fifteen and thirty-five may be brought before a judge by any person and charged with being idle and dissolute. A parent or guardian could charge a woman under 21 years with incorrigible. This section was enacted in 1919. (*Female Refuges Act, SOR* 1937, c. 384.)

CHAPTER 6

1 Some children were put into homes by social workers under powers of the Minister of Public Welfare. Other children went to homes through the Juvenile Court, later called Family Court. It was a bone of contention for children placed by social workers for being neglected in the same institutions with those who had committed offences and gone through court. "Liable to grow up to be idle and dissolute" was a definition of a neglected child.

There was one appeal under the *Female Refuges Act* in 1930. Violet Hypatia Bower, 22 years old, the mother of two illegitimate children (one died at birth) requested her freedom. Sentenced to the Belmont Home, she was transferred to the Hospital for the Insane at Cobourg. Two medical doctors appointed by her father stated she was not insane. The judge stated that immorality was a symptom of insanity. The appeal was denied.

CHAPTER 11

1 "Girls' Jail Shocks Grand Jury: Secret Visit to Toronto Dungeons. The Grand Jury stated, 'The detention cells of this 19th century building are approximately 4' x 7', the iron beds have a mesh kind of spring, and underneath is the chamber pot." (*Toronto Star* November 3, 1964.)

CHAPTER 12

1 "We still had the building and a group of eighteen women, varying in age from fifty to seventy years who were sent to us from all parts of the province long before we were placed under the Industrial Refuge Act in 1917" (*Annual Report*, October 1939, The Toronto Industrial Refuge and The Aged Women's Home and The Aged Men's Home).
2 "I would like to report another term of very excellent health among the inmates" (Dr. Isabel Ayer, *Annual Report of Toronto Industrial Refuge*, October 1939, 24).

CHAPTER 15

1 According to the act respecting British Nationality, Naturalization, and Aliens, "the wife of a British subject shall be deemed to be a British subject, and the wife of an alien shall be deemed to be an alien" (*National Status of Married Women and Infant Children, SOR* 1927, c. 138, s. 13).

CHAPTER 18

1 "Girls Cry When Leaving Refuge for Reformatory," *Toronto Daily Star* July 19, 1939; "Close Refuge, Housed Girls for 85 Years," *Globe and Mail* July 19, 1939.

2 Miss Milne was convinced that the Mercer Reformatory could rehabilitate women. In her annual report in 1939 she said that "terms under six months are too short to enable us to do enough towards fitting them to become respectable citizens." She believed the women were receptive to Christian salvation.

3 A.L. McKay, "Incidence and Treatment of Veneral Disease in Ontario Reformatories," *The Canadian Public Health Journal* vol. 14 (1923): 558-59.

4 Serological Report (No. 15630) dealt solely with the weekly treatment by the drugs sulphanilamide and Dagenan. These drugs were still in the experimental stage and a patient needed constant monitoring. I have to believe that blood samples were being taken but I was unaware of this due to cauterizing of the wounds. Even if I hadn't been in severe pain, it's unlikely I would have been able to see what was happening. The report was signed by the director of laboratories. It mentioned that a "soothing antiseptic" was being used.

According to the 1939 Ontario Medical Association's *Formulary*, Dagenan was "for use in Lobar Pneumonia ONLY" (32). Sulphanilamide was not to be supplied for the treatment of veneral disease.

ACKNOWLEDGEMENTS

For his political acuity and fight against injustice, I strongly admire Harry Kopyto, legal consultant, and the Friends of Velma, who rallied for justice for women imprisoned under Ontario's iniquitous Female Refuges Act. Many others through the Friends of Velma expressed their concern for the hundreds or thousands of women wrongfully convicted under the Female Refuges Act. Good-hearted Donna Cheung-Tam provided generous financial assistance to launch the Friends of Velma Committee.

I am grateful to the Ontario NDP Caucus for presenting me with the J.S. Woodsworth award for anti-racism in 2002 at the International Day for the Elimination of Racial Discrimination.

David Midanik, my lawyer, endured my erratic behaviour for two years during negotiations for compensation with two Ontario governments. I am grateful to David Suzuki for his sympathy and encouragement.

Rosemary Aubert, author of a series of *Ellis Portal Mysteries*, edited my book in its early stages and gave me confidence. I also cherish the encouragement and assistance of Geoffrey Reaume, author of *Remembrance of Patients Past: Patient Life at the Toronto Hospital for the Insane, 1870-1940*. I am indebted to June Callwood for her suggestions and encouragement during her period as writer-in-residence at the Toronto Reference Library.

I sincerely recognize the dedication of Professor Constance Backhouse, author of several books including *Petticoats and Prejudice: Women and the Law in Nineteenth-Century Canada*, and *Colour-Coded: A Legal History of Racism in Canada, 1900-1950*. Professor Backhouse has presented aspects of my case in a legal forum.

My gratitude for their personal involvement with me in presenting my story extends to Professors Karen Dubinski and Renata Mohr as well as lawyer Kiki Roach.

Thank you to the Ontario Elizabeth Fry Society for inviting me to speak at annual meetings and for writing glowing reports in their newsletters. I also appreciate the efforts of Nancy Webb to to equate my story with other women in conflict with the law.

Joseph Markin, lawyer, successfully obtained Intervenor Status for me under Chief Justice Roy McMurtry in the Sandra Murray appeal to the Supreme Court of Canada. The appeal was against the decision by Judge Coo that no court proceedings could be instituted for anything that happened before September 1, 1963.

I'm grateful for the support of Josie Macpherson, Coordinator of Survivors of Medical Abuse, who introduced my story to her history class.

I would like to thank the following journalists for their sympathetic presentation of my case: Michele Landsberg of the *Toronto Star*, Jan Wong and Michael Valpy of the *Globe and Mail*, Shirley Chan of *Ming Pao* Newspapers (Canada) Ltd., and Bernadette Colonego of *Ausland* in Switzerland.

Appreciation also goes to the staff at the Archives of Ontario for their generous assistance, especially Sharon Fleming, Jim Lewis, Judith Emery, Cathy Hawkins, Jack Choules, Stormie Stewart, and Maria Babic.

I was fortunate in having Jacqueline Larson of Wilfrid Laurier University Press as editor of this book.

Books in the Life Writing Series Published by Wilfrid Laurier University Press